This book is lovingly dedicated to my Dad –
without his caring support I would never have
survived my teen years.

———∘●∘———

Good Luck

&

Best Wishes to You

Acknowledgments

Again I thank my friends and family for their support and for tasting my recipes and giving me honest feedback. I thank my loving husband for believing in me and for all the hours he has worked on typing, formatting, and all the other things I don't even know about.

Thanks to Gopher State Litho for putting my book together so beautifully. Gopher States' Jim Meyer, David Swanson, and Steve Lange all did a great job of making this work. Kudos to Shaf, D.B. Shafer for his great job on photography. I want to thank Nancy Sawyer and all the wonderful folks at Post Haste, Inc. for making sure every order is shipped.

Also many thanks to the thousands of people who have purchased my first book *Eat Yourself Thin Like I Did*. I hope this book will help you to achieve the success you desire.

Nancy Moshier

EAT YOURSELF

THIN

WITH FABULOUS

DESSERTS

SUGAR FREE
LOW CARB
RECIPES

BY

NANCY MOSHIER, RN

EAT YOURSELF THIN WITH FABULOUS DESSERTS

Published by:
Nancy's Cookbooks, Inc.
P.O. Box 338
Garrison, MN 56450

Second cookbook in the Eat Yourself Thin series.
Printed at Gopher State Litho
3232 East 40th Street, Minneapolis, MN. 55406 USA
Cover design by David Swanson.

Second printing.
Printed in the United States of America.

Library of Congress Control Number: 2002105049

ISBN: 0-9701029-1-7

Introduction

This is my second book in a series of low carb cookbooks. My hope is that I may help others achieve the success I have had living the low carb way of life. I have been extremely overweight most of my life. I had a couple of short intervals where I lost a lot of weight, only to gain it back faster than I lost it, plus a few extra pounds. Most every weight-loss diet leaves you hungry and feeling deprived. The majority of people can only tolerate constant hunger for a limited time, that's just human nature. I can honestly say that I have never been hungry on the Atkins Diet, because when you are hungry you can eat. It's just that simple. I started the Atkins Diet in July of 1998 and have been living the low carb way of life ever since. I feel better than I have ever felt in my life. It has caused my fibromyalgia to go into remission and my total cholesterol and triglycerides to drop dramatically.

To date I have lost 130 pounds and have been able to stay at my present weight for over 2 years. I know I will never be overweight again. I truly believe the only difficult part is making the commitment to yourself, that you are going to do this for life and you will not let anything or anyone cause you to break that commitment. There are many plateaus on low carb diets but while you are not losing weight you are getting smaller. I even had one plateau that lasted 5 months. I am positive that if I had not made that firm commitment to myself, that I would not go off this diet no matter what the scale read, or anything else, for that matter, I would probably have gotten discouraged and gone off it. But I refused to get discouraged and just kept on keeping on. I only lost 3 pounds during those 5 months but I went from a size 16 to a size 12. I was a size 24 when I started. I am now a size 10 and can wear some size 8's.

One of my Physicians explained to me how I could drop 2 dress sizes and only lose 3 pounds. She said, and I quote, " a pound of fat is big and fluffy, while a pound of muscle is small and compact, but they still both weigh a pound. This is the only diet that is muscle sparing. On any other type of diet you will lose fat *and* muscle. And remember, your heart is a muscle." So if you think about it logically, those 3 pounds I lost were the big, fluffy fat pounds and that is why I was 2 sizes smaller.

I'm sure you will find people that make totally irresponsible statements about eating low carbs. The most common one is that it will "damage your kidneys." This simply is not true. Dr. Atkins states, "Too many people believe this untruth simply because it has been repeated so often that even intelligent health professionals assume it must have been reported somewhere. But the fact is that it has never been reported anywhere. I have yet to see someone produce a study for me to review, or even cite a specific case in which a protein-containing diet causes any form of a kidney disorder."[1]

If you have kidney disease or damaged kidneys you should not go on low carbs. But if you have normal healthy kidneys and drink the 8 glasses of water a day that you should always drink, your kidneys will be unaffected. After two and a half years on low carbs I was so tired of hearing that my kidneys were going to be damaged that I had an IVP (kidney x-rays with dye) and kidney function tests. The results were all normal. I can't help but wonder where these people get their misinformation.

My husband who has lost 80 pounds on Atkins urged me to create these recipes and write this book. His biggest problem with any diet has always been his love of desserts and basically anything sweet. We were both on a low-fat diet for over 5 years and we both gained weight. Our total cholesterol and triglycerides were sky high. We ate pasta with my homemade low-fat sauce, lots of bread without butter, corn on the cob with the tiniest bit of margarine spray (yuk), baked potatoes with fat-free sour cream, fat-free ice cream bars, fat-free baked goods, etc. We now know why we gained weight because fat doesn't make you fat, sugar/carbohydrates make you fat. We also know that if you follow the low carb way of life you *can eat fat.* You can eat butter, heavy whipping cream, olive oil, bacon, eggs, and your HDL (good) cholesterol will go up and your triglycerides will go down. I personally believe the *low-fat diet* is responsible for the obesity epidemic we are experiencing now.

You must understand though that this is not a diet you can go off and back on. If you cheat you will probably gain weight. And what's more, your body has to get back to the fat-burning mode, so it sets you back, sometimes a whole week. It isn't worth it; nothing tastes good enough to let it set you back. With meals from my first book and desserts from this book why would anyone ever need to cheat?

---

[1] Dr. Atkins Completely Updated New Edition New Diet Revolution, printed 2002

I just want to mention that exercise makes a big difference in your weight loss. I couldn't even walk for exercise until I had lost 45 pounds, it just hurt too much. But when I was able to start walking, it really revved up my metabolism.

I am so thankful that I have found a way to lose the weight for life and get healthy in the process. I have dedicated my life to helping those who are in the shape I was in. I felt helpless and hopeless and I truly thought it was my destiny to be fat and miserable and in horrific pain from fibromyalgia. Every morning it took me at least 20 minutes to get out of bed. No matter what your situation is you are not helpless or hopeless, I am living proof of that. Remember the only hard part is making the commitment to yourself. Then buy one of the low carb diet books, I personally recommend Atkins, and read it thoroughly so you understand how it works and what kinds of foods you can eat and the number of carbs you can have. Be sure to read the entire book. The rest is a breeze. Best of luck to you - I know you can do it and I hope you enjoy the desserts I have created for you.

Nancy Moshier

Helpful Hints

Toasting Nuts:

The easiest way to toast nuts is on a microwave safe plate. Microwave on high for 1 minute, stir, and then repeat this two or three more times until nuts give off a toasted fragrance. You can also toast on a cookie sheet in a 350° oven for about 6-8 minutes, stirring halfway through. Watch closely so they don't get too dark or burn. They can also be toasted in a dry skillet over medium heat, stirring constantly until they give off a toasted fragrance. This just takes a few minutes. I toast and chop a large amount at a time and freeze them, double bagged, ready to use at a moment's notice. Be sure to cool completely, then chop.

Pressing Crusts into Pans:

The easiest way to press dough into pans is to use the thumb side of your hand. You may have to use fingers a little when nearly finished but the side of your hand works best up to that point. Spray your hands so the dough doesn't stick to them. Sometimes the dough is a little stickier than other times probably due to humidity changes. If it is too sticky, add another tablespoon or two of shake mix, it will hardly affect carb count.

Freezing Citrus Zest:

Orange, Lemon, and Lime Zest freeze wonderfully. When I am grating zest for a recipe, I grate a lot of it and freeze it in 1-teaspoon packets in a lock-top bag. Cut up small pieces of plastic wrap and wrap each teaspoon of zest. Label and date the bag. Saves you time and it thaws quickly.

Baking Parchment:

One of the best tips I can give you for baking is to line all your pans with baking parchment. Virtually ***nothing*** sticks to parchment. It can be re-used several times and you can cut some pieces to fit your pans so you don't have to cut them every time you bake. Just trace around the outside bottom of your pan with a pencil, then cut inside the lines. It used to be hard to find baking parchment but now Reynolds makes it and you can find it at Wal-Mart among the plastic wrap and aluminum foil.

Water:

I know it is difficult for some people to get their 8 glasses of water in everyday. I cannot emphasize enough how important this is though. I have found the easiest way to accomplish this is to fill a pitcher with 64 oz. of water (8 – 8 oz. glasses) in the morning and keep filling your glass from the pitcher until it's empty. If you still have water in the pitcher at the end of the day, you know what you have to do before you go to bed.

Carb Counting Books:

I strongly urge you to purchase 2 carb counting books. You need to know how many carbs you are eating in order to be successful. These are very comprehensive books and if one doesn't list something, usually the other one does. These are *The Complete Book of Food Counts* by Corrine T. Netzer and *Carbohydrates, Calories & Fat* by Dr. Art Ulene. The carb counts of my recipes are accurate to the best of my knowledge. I have used USDA charts, both carb-counting books listed above, and manufacturers labels to figure carb counts.

Measurements and Weights

1 teaspoon . . . . 1/3 tablespoon

1 tablespoon . . . . 3 teaspoons

2 tablespoons . . . . 1 fluid ounce

4 tablespoons . . . . 1/4 cup or 2 ounces

8 tablespoons . . . . 1/2 cup or 4 ounces

16 tablespoons . . . . 1 cup or 8 ounces

1/4 cup . . . . 4 tablespoons

1/3 cup . . . . 5 tablespoons + 1 teaspoon

1/2 cup . . . . 8 tablespoons

1 cup . . . . 1/2 pint or 8 ounces

2 cups . . . . 1 pint or 16 ounces

1 quart . . . . 2 pints or 4 cups

1 gallon . . . . 4 quarts

1 pound . . . . 16 ounces

Contents

ASSORTED DESSERTS & TREATS

Almond Crunch Banana Cheesecake

Beautiful and delicious - an elegant dessert for a dinner party

Almond Crunch:

1/4 cup sliced almonds
1 tablespoon butter, melted
1 tablespoon Splenda® sweetener

Preheat oven to 350°. Line a shallow baking pan with aluminum foil and then spray. In a small bowl mix butter and Splenda®. Add almonds and stir gently until well coated. Spread almonds on foil in a single layer. Bake 4-5 minutes watching closely so they don't get too dark. Remove from oven and set aside to cool. Leave oven at 350°.

Crust:

1 - recipe Vanilla Cookie Crust, (page 92) do not bake.

Butter a 7" spring form pan and then line the sides and bottom with cooking parchment. Do not skip parchment or it will stick. Pat the dough into the pan covering the bottom and up the sides. Cover the outside bottom and up the sides with aluminum foil. Bake 8 minutes and then cool on a rack. Reduce oven to 325°.

Continued on next page.

Filling:

2 - 8 oz. packages cream cheese, softened
3 tablespoons butter, softened
1/4 cup heavy whipping cream
2 teaspoons banana extract
1/3 cup plus 1 tablespoon Splenda® sweetener
1 tablespoon sugar-free Jell-O® instant banana pudding mix
2 large eggs, yolks broken

While crust is cooling prepare filling. In a medium bowl beat cream cheese with an electric mixer until smooth and fluffy. Add remaining ingredients except eggs and beat until smooth. Add eggs and mix on low until just incorporated. Do not over mix. Pour into cooled crust (make sure crust is completely cooled) and rap gently on counter to release air bubbles. Break up almonds into even pieces and sprinkle evenly over top of cheesecake. Bake for 1 hour or until barely set. Turn oven off and let cheesecake cool in oven 1 hour. Finish cooling at room temperature on a rack. Refrigerate at least 6 hours before serving. Do not remove sides of pan until <u>completely cooled</u>. Cut into 8 equal pieces. Store covered in the refrigerator.

8 Servings at 5.2 grams carbs each

Apricot Surprise Muffins
Great with coffee or tea for a yummy treat

Topping:
4 oz. cream cheese, softened (1/2 of an 8 oz. package)
1/4 cup low carb apricot fruit spread (2 grams carbs per 1 tablespoon)

In a small bowl combine cream cheese and fruit spread until thoroughly mixed and then set aside.

Muffin Batter:
1/4 cup blanched almond flour
3 tablespoons Atkins® bake mix
1/3 cup Splenda® sweetener
1 teaspoon baking powder
1/8 teaspoon salt
5 large eggs, separated
1/2 teaspoon cream of tartar
1/3 cup heavy whipping cream
2 tablespoons butter, melted
2 teaspoons vanilla extract

Preheat oven to 350°. Butter and spray a 12-cup regular size nonstick muffin pan and then set aside. In a medium mixing bowl whisk together first 5 ingredients until well combined and then set aside. Place egg whites and cream of tartar in a large mixing bowl and then set aside. In a small bowl or measuring cup whisk together egg yolks, cream, melted butter, and extract until well combined. Whisk cream mixture into dry mixture until smooth and then set aside. Whip egg whites with an electric mixer until stiff but not dry. Gently fold batter into egg whites being careful not to deflate whites. Divide evenly into prepared muffin pan. Top each muffin with apricot mixture dividing evenly. Bake about 25 minutes or until lightly browned and muffin springs back when lightly touched with a finger. Cool on a rack. Store covered in the refrigerator. Best when served cold.

12 Servings at 2.8 grams carbs each

Blueberry Cream Tart

On a scale of 1-10 my "tasters" rated this one an 11.
It also makes a beautiful presentation!

Crust:
1 - recipe Vanilla Cookie Crust dough, (page 92) unbaked

Press dough into a sprayed 10" tart pan or deep dish pie pan and then bake as directed and cool on a rack.

Topping:
1   pint fresh blueberries (if unavailable use unsweetened frozen)
1/4   cup Splenda® sweetener
1/8   teaspoon guar gum

Wash and sort berries. Transfer to a small nonstick saucepan. Stir in Splenda® and guar gum. Do not add water. The water clinging to the berries is sufficient. Cook over low heat uncovered for 10-15 minutes stirring occasionally until sauce is thickened and berries are cooked down a bit. Remove from heat, transfer to a plastic bowl and cool to room temperature. You can speed this up by placing plastic bowl in the refrigerator. While topping is cooling prepare the filling.

Filling:
2   cups heavy whipping cream
2   tablespoons sugar-free Jell-O® instant vanilla pudding mix
1   teaspoon vanilla extract
1/4   cup Splenda® sweetener

In a medium mixing bowl combine all filling ingredients and whip with an electric mixer until stiff. Spread evenly over cooled crust then top evenly with cooled berry topping. Take care spreading the topping so the filling doesn't get mixed in it. It would still taste great but wouldn't be as pretty. Refrigerate at least 2 hours. Cut into 10 equal pieces. Store covered in the refrigerator.

10 Servings at 9.4 grams carbs each

Bread Pudding

It just doesn't get any better than this and low carb too

6 slices cinnamon raisin Keto® bread, cubed and left out to dry about 2 hours
8 large eggs
1 1/2 cups heavy whipping cream
1 1/2 cups water
2/3 cup Splenda® sweetener, divided
1 1/2 teaspoons liquid Sweet'N Low® sweetener
1 teaspoon vanilla extract
2 tablespoons cold butter
1 1/2 teaspoons ground cinnamon

Preheat oven to 350º. Butter a 9"x13" nonstick cake pan. Spread bread cubes evenly in prepared pan. In a large bowl whisk eggs, cream, water, 1/3 cup of Splenda®, Sweet'N Low®, and vanilla extract until thoroughly combined. Pour mixture over bread cubes pushing bread down so all is covered with egg mixture. In a small bowl mix remaining 1/3 cup of Splenda® and cinnamon together. Sprinkle evenly over top. Dot with butter and cover with aluminum foil. Bake 45 minutes, remove foil and bake 10 more minutes. Cut into 15 equal pieces. Serve warm or cold. Store covered in the refrigerator.

Note: This is especially good topped with Vanilla Sauce (page 38). Be sure to count the carbs in the sauce.

15 Servings at 3.9 grams carbs each

Brownies
Chocolate bliss and even better frosted
with Chocolate Twist® spread

1/2 - 1 oz. square unsweetened baking chocolate
1/2 cup butter, softened (1 stick)
1 cup Carb Solutions® chocolate shake mix
1/4 cup heavy whipping cream
1/4 cup water
2 teaspoons vanilla extract
1/2 cup Splenda® sweetener
1 tablespoon baking powder
3 large eggs
1/4 cup walnuts, toasted and chopped small
3 tablespoons sugar-free Chocolate Twist® spread (optional)

Preheat oven to 350°. Butter and spray a 7"x11" nonstick baking pan and then set aside. In a small bowl melt baking chocolate in the microwave for about 40 seconds, stopping and stirring after 20 seconds. Do not overheat or over stir. In a medium bowl cream butter and melted chocolate together. Add next 6 ingredients and beat by hand until smooth. Add eggs one at a time and beat well after each. Stir in walnuts until evenly distributed. Spread evenly in prepared pan. Bake for about 25 minutes or until springs back when lightly touched with a finger. When cool frost with Chocolate Twist® if desired. Cut into 24 equal pieces. Store covered in the refrigerator.

24 Servings at 1.7 grams carbs each unfrosted

24 Servings at 1.8 grams carbs each frosted

Butterscotch Mousse Tarts With Warm Praline Sauce

You can make everything the day before and assemble just before serving for a scrumptious and elegant dessert.

Tart Shells:
1 - recipe Vanilla Cookie Crust (page 92), do not press into pie pan.

Preheat oven to 375°. Turn upside down and spray the <u>underside</u> of a 12 count nonstick mini muffin pan. Divide dough into 12 equal pieces. Shape each piece into a ball and flatten between palms of hands. Pat over bottom and down sides of each upside down muffin cup. Place upside down muffin pan in oven and bake for 10-12 minutes. Cool 5 minutes then carefully remove each tart shell from pan and cool on a rack. Store covered in the refrigerator until needed.

Filling:
2 cups heavy whipping cream
3 tablespoons Brown Sugar Twin® sweetener
2 tablespoons sugar-free Jell-O® instant butterscotch pudding mix
1 teaspoon vanilla extract
1 tablespoon butter, softened

In a medium mixing bowl combine filling ingredients in order given and whip with an electric mixer until stiff. Refrigerate covered until needed.

Continued on next page.

Praline Sauce:

1/4 cup butter

1/4 cup pecans, toasted and chopped small

3 tablespoons Brown Sugar Twin® sweetener

1 tablespoon Splenda® sweetener

1/4 cup heavy whipping cream

In a small saucepan combine all sauce ingredients. Cook over medium low heat to boiling, stirring constantly. Reduce heat to low and continue to boil 4-5 minutes, stirring occasionally. Remove from heat and let cool until just warm. If not using immediately refrigerate covered. To reheat, place in a microwave safe bowl and heat on low just until room temperature stopping and stirring every 10 seconds. Do not overheat or heat on high or the sauce will separate. If it does separate, let cool a bit and beat with a fork until it re-incorporates and becomes creamy again.

To Assemble:

Just before serving divide filling evenly between tart shells. Place on dessert plates and top with sauce, dividing sauce evenly. Serve immediately. Store covered and refrigerate leftovers.

12 Servings at 3.4 grams carbs each

Chocolate Chunk Blonde Brownies

A wonderful treat and so low in carbs

1/2 cup butter, softened (1 stick)
1/4 cup Splenda® sweetener
1 tablespoon sugar-free Jell-O® instant butterscotch pudding mix
2 tablespoons Brown Sugar Twin® sweetener
1/4 cup heavy whipping cream
1/4 cup water
1 cup Carb Solutions® vanilla shake mix
1 tablespoon baking powder
2 teaspoons vanilla extract
3 large eggs
1/4 cup walnuts, toasted and chopped small
2 Ross® chocolate dark delight candy bars, chopped the size of
chocolate chips.

Preheat oven to 350º. Butter and spray a 7"x11" nonstick baking pan and then set aside. In a medium bowl cream together first 4 ingredients. Whisk in cream, water, shake mix, baking powder, and vanilla extract. Whisk in eggs one at a time completely incorporating each egg. Stir in walnuts and chocolate pieces. Scrape into prepared pan and smooth top. Bake for about 25 minutes or until lightly browned and springs back when lightly touched with a finger. Cool in pan on a rack. When completely cool cut into 24 equal pieces. Store covered in the refrigerator.

24 Servings at 1.3 grams carbs each

Chocolate Drizzle

Dresses up any dessert while only adding 1 gram of carbs. Fantastic!

1 Ross® dark delight chocolate bar

In a glass custard cup or small bowl melt broken up bar for 1 minute in the microwave on high until just melted, stopping and stirring at 30 seconds. Place a small plastic sandwich bag in a small juice glass, forcing the point of one corner to bottom of glass. Fold the remaining plastic bag over the outside of the glass. Scrape the melted chocolate into the bag aiming for the corner. Remove the bag from the glass and with your fingers on the outside of the bag, force as much of the chocolate into the corner as you can. Twist the bag just above the frosting and you now have a mini disposable decorating bag. Snip the tiniest bit off the corner and drizzle chocolate in a back and forth motion across dessert. Then turn and drizzle back and forth in the other direction so you will have a criss cross pattern. Hold the bag over the dessert as you snip the corner, it will start running immediately. This looks beautiful and really adds to the overall taste.

1 gram of carbs

Chocolate Fudge

Creamy, smooth, melt in your mouth fudge
and it's so quick and easy.

1 cup heavy whipping cream
8 oz. american cheese, cut in cubes (do not use "cheese spread" such as Velveeta®)
1 cup unsalted butter, (2 sticks) No substitutions, must be unsalted
2 - 1 oz. squares unsweetened baking chocolate, broken up
2 cups Splenda® sweetener
1 teaspoon liquid Sweet'N Low® sweetener
1 tablespoon unsweetened baking cocoa, sifted
1 tablespoon vanilla extract
1/2 cup walnuts, toasted and chopped small (optional)

Spray an 8" square baking pan and then set aside. In a medium heavy saucepan combine first 6 ingredients and cook over medium heat stirring frequently until melted. Sift in cocoa and bring to a boil. Boil stirring constantly for 1 minute. Remove from heat and add extract and walnuts. Pour into a plastic bowl and let cool until barely warm, whisking occasionally. It is cool enough when butter no longer separates. When butter stays incorporated pour into prepared pan, smooth top and refrigerate several hours or until cold and firm. Cut into 64 equal pieces. Store covered in the refrigerator.

64 Servings at 1.2 grams carbs each (without walnuts)

64 Servings at 1.4 grams carbs each (with walnuts)

Chocolate Ice Cream Cups

Quick and easy to make and oh so good.
Great to have on hand for a chocolate attack

1 cup heavy whipping cream
1 1/2 teaspoons chocolate extract
1 teaspoon vanilla extract
1 1/4 teaspoons liquid Sweet'N Low® sweetener
1/4 cup Splenda® sweetener
2 tablespoons Carb Solutions® chocolate shake mix
8 oz. cream cheese, softened
1 tablespoon unsweetened baking cocoa
2 tablespoons sugar-free Chocolate Twist® spread

In a medium mixing bowl whip cream, extracts, sweeteners, and shake mix with an electric mixer until thick but not stiff and then set aside. In another medium bowl whip cream cheese, cocoa, and chocolate spread until smooth and fluffy. Add whipped cream mixture and whip just until well combined. Spoon 1/2 cup into each of 11 small paper cups. Place a wooden stick into each if desired. Freeze on a cookie sheet until solid and then store in a zip-top bag in the freezer.

Note: If you put sticks in them remove from freezer when ready to eat. Then just roll in your hands to warm a little bit and peel off paper. Without sticks, either let set until starting to soften or place in the microwave for 15-30 seconds.

11 Servings at 5 grams carbs each

Chocolate Mousse

Light and luscious. A perfect end to any meal and so easy to make

2 Ross® chocolate dark delight candy bars
2 cups heavy whipping cream
2 teaspoons vanilla extract
2 teaspoons chocolate extract
1/4 cup Splenda® sweetener
1 teaspoon liquid Sweet'N Low® sweetener

In a small glass bowl break candy bars into chunks and microwave just until melted, 1-2 minutes stopping and stirring every 30 seconds. Cool to room temperature. In a medium mixing bowl combine all ingredients except cooled chocolate and whip with an electric mixer until it starts to thicken. While mixer is running, add cooled chocolate and whip until thick. Do not over beat or you will have chocolate butter. Chocolate will tend to clump if you do not add it with the mixer running. Divide evenly into 8 – 1/2 cup servings. Store covered in the refrigerator.

8 Servings at 2.2 grams carbs each

Creamy Frosted Jell-O Squares

Great for days when you have eaten most of your carb limit but still want dessert. Less than 1 gram of carbs per serving. This is even okay for Atkins induction.

Jell-O® Layer:

12 oz. cream cheese, softened (1 1/2 - 8 oz. packages)
2 small boxes sugar-free Jell-O®, any flavor
1 cup boiling water
2 3/4 cups cold water

Spray a 9" square cake pan and then set aside. In a large mixing bowl beat softened cream cheese with an electric mixer until smooth and fluffy and then set aside. In a medium bowl dissolve both packages of Jell-O® in boiling water stirring until completely dissolved. Gradually beat hot Jell-O® into cream cheese until smooth. Stir in cold water and mix well. Pour into prepared pan and chill until set.

Topping:

1/2 cup heavy whipping cream
1/4 teaspoon vanilla extract
30 drops liquid Sweet'N Low® sweetener
1 teaspoon Splenda® sweetener

In a small bowl whip all topping ingredients with an electric mixer until thick and spreadable. Spread evenly over Jell-O® after Jell-O® is set. Cut into 16 equal pieces. Store covered in the refrigerator.

16 Servings at .8 grams carbs each

Crème Filled Chocolate Horns

All I can say about these is WOW!

Chocolate Pancakes:

2 large eggs, separated
1/4 teaspoon cream of tartar
1/2 cup heavy whipping cream
1/2 cup water
1 tablespoon baking powder
3 tablespoons butter, melted
1 tablespoon unsweetened cocoa
2/3 cup Carb Solutions® chocolate shake mix
1 tablespoon Splenda® sweetener
Dash salt

In a medium bowl place egg whites and cream of tartar and then set aside. In a small bowl or custard cup melt butter in microwave about 15-30 seconds. Stir in cocoa and then set aside. In a large bowl whisk egg yolks, cocoa mixture and remaining ingredients (except egg whites) until thoroughly mixed and then set aside. Whip egg whites with an electric mixer until stiff but not dry. Gently fold chocolate mixture into egg whites being careful not to deflate whites. Heat a nonstick griddle over medium heat. Wipe griddle with an oil soaked paper towel. Griddle is hot enough when a drop of water skitters on it. Drop batter by 1/2 cupfuls onto griddle. Turn when top begins to look dry. Continue to cook until done, about 30-60 seconds. Fold in half and cool on a rack.

Crème Filling:

1 cup heavy whipping cream
1 tablespoon sugar-free Jell-O® instant white chocolate pudding mix
1/2 teaspoon vanilla extract
2 tablespoons Splenda® sweetener

In a medium bowl whip all ingredients with an electric mixer until stiff. Do not over beat or it will turn to butter.

Assembly:

When cool, cut chocolate pancakes in half along crease. Spread 2 1/2 tablespoons filling on bottom third of each half-round. Roll into a cone shape, pushing filling to near top. Seal with a dab of filling. Store covered in the refrigerator.

10 Servings at 3.2 grams carbs each

Fruit Dessert Pizza

If you have tasted the high carb version of this dessert then you will be thrilled to find that this is even better!

Crust:

1/2 cup Carb Solutions® vanilla shake mix
2 tablespoons Brown Sugar Twin® sweetener
1/2 teaspoon xanthan gum
3/4 cup heavy whipping cream
2 large eggs
1 teaspoon vanilla extract

Preheat oven to 350º. Butter a 10"x14" nonstick baking pan with sides, spray well and then set aside. In a small mixing bowl whisk together dry ingredients. Whisk in cream, eggs, and extract until smooth and then set aside for 10 minutes to thicken. After 10 minutes spread crust mixture evenly into prepared pan. Bake for about 15 minutes or until set and lightly browned. Cool in pan on a rack.

Topping:

1 cup unsweetened fresh or frozen blueberries
6 tablespoons Splenda® sweetener, divided
1 cup fresh strawberries, sliced
1 large kiwi fruit, peeled and sliced crosswise into 1/4" slices

While crust is baking rinse and sort blueberries and then transfer to a small, heavy nonstick saucepan. Stir in 3 tablespoons Splenda® and cook over low heat stirring occasionally until syrupy and berries are soft, about 10-15 minutes. Do not add water. Water clinging to berries is sufficient. Pour into a plastic bowl and then set aside to cool. In a small bowl gently stir remaining 3 tablespoons Splenda® into strawberries and refrigerate until needed. Keep kiwi refrigerated until needed.

Filling:

8 oz. cream cheese, softened
3/4 cup heavy whipping cream, whipped just until thick
1/2 cup Splenda® sweetener
1 teaspoon vanilla extract

In a medium mixing bowl beat cream cheese with an electric mixer until smooth and fluffy. Beat in whipped cream, Splenda®, and extract just until well blended. Spread evenly over cooled crust then chill until filling is set, about 30-45 minutes. Top evenly with kiwi and strawberries in an attractive pattern. Drizzle blueberry sauce evenly over top. Cut into 18 equal pieces. Store covered in the refrigerator.

18 Servings at 4.9 grams carbs each

Macadamia Nut Truffles

Fabulous melt-in-your-mouth truffles that everyone is crazy about

1 - recipe Chocolate Fudge Sauce (page 38)
1/4 cup butter, softened
40 whole macadamia nuts

Stir butter into Chocolate Fudge Sauce until completely combined. Chill until firm.

Coating:
3 tablespoons Splenda® sweetener
1 tablespoon Carb Solutions® chocolate shake mix
1 teaspoon unsweetened cocoa

In a small shallow dish mix coating ingredients until thoroughly combined.

Divide firm chocolate into 40 even pieces. Mold each piece around a macadamia nut and shape into a ball. Roll each ball in coating and shake off excess. Work quickly so the chocolate doesn't melt. Better yet, recruit a helper if you can. Refrigerate until firm with waxed paper or plastic wrap between layers in a tightly covered container. Discard any remaining coating. Should be about 2 1/2 tablespoons left. Store covered in the refrigerator.

40 Servings at 1.1 grams carbs each

Maple Walnut Creams

These creamy, yummy candies are sure to please

8 oz. cream cheese, softened
1/2 cup butter, softened (1 stick)
1 cup heavy whipping cream
4 tablespoons sugar-free Jell-O® instant butterscotch pudding mix, divided
1/2 cup Splenda® sweetener, divided
1 teaspoon maple flavoring
1/4 cup walnuts, toasted and finely chopped

In a small mixing bowl combine 1/4 cup Splenda®, 3 tablespoons pudding mix, and all other above ingredients until well combined. Refrigerate at least 1 hour covered. When firm shape into 64 small balls. Place on waxed paper.

Coating:

4 1/2 tablespoons walnuts, toasted and ground
1 tablespoon remaining pudding mix
1/4 cup remaining Splenda® sweetener

In a shallow dish mix coating ingredients until well combined. Roll balls in coating and store covered in the refrigerator.

64 candies at .7 grams carbs each

Marmalade Muffins

Wonderful muffins remind me of sunshine.
Great for a morning coffee break

5 large eggs, separated
1/2 teaspoon cream of tartar
1/4 cup heavy whipping cream
1/4 cup low carb orange marmalade fruit spread
     (1 tablespoon/2 grams carbs)
2 tablespoons butter, melted and cooled
1 teaspoon orange zest, grated (orange part only)
1/2 teaspoon orange extract
2 tablespoons Atkins® bake mix
3 tablespoons blanched almond flour
1/3 cup Splenda® sweetener
1 teaspoon baking powder
1/8 teaspoon salt

Preheat oven to 350º. Butter and spray a 12-cup nonstick regular size muffin pan and then set aside. In a large mixing bowl place egg whites and cream of tartar and then set aside. In a medium mixing bowl whisk together egg yolks, cream, fruit spread, melted butter, orange zest, and extract. Whisk in remaining ingredients (except egg whites) until smooth and then set aside. Whip egg whites with an electric mixer until stiff but not dry. Gently fold batter into egg whites, taking care not to deflate whites. Divide evenly into prepared muffin pan. Bake about 25 minutes or until lightly browned and springs back when lightly touched with a finger. Cool on a rack 10 minutes before removing from pan and then cool to room temperature on a rack Store covered in the refrigerator. Best when served cold.

12 Servings at 2.3 grams carbs each

Meringue Shells

Light and crispy – these are great with any filling

5 large egg whites
1/2 teaspoon cream of tartar
1/2 cup Splenda® sweetener
1 1/2 teaspoons vanilla extract

Preheat oven to 425°. Spray the underside of a 12-cup regular size nonstick muffin pan and then set aside. In a large mixing bowl whip egg whites, cream of tartar, and vanilla extract with an electric mixer until frothy. Add Splenda® 1 tablespoon at a time while continuing to whip until very stiff and slightly shiny. Spoon evenly over the underside of each muffin cup, shaping with a spoon or spatula. Bake about 15 minutes or until lightly browned and crisp. Cool on a rack. Carefully remove each shell. Fill with Chocolate Mousse (page 22) or berries and top with sweetened whipped cream, or any desired filling.

Note: Be sure to add carb count of desired filling to each serving.

12 Servings at 1 gram carbs each

Mocha Meringue Bars

Super treats and the chocolaty crust tastes great with the mocha meringue

2 tablespoons boiling water
2 tablespoons unsweetened baking cocoa
1 teaspoon instant coffee
1 2/3 cups Carb Solutions® chocolate shake mix
3/4 cup butter, softened (1 1/2 sticks)
4 large egg whites
1/4 teaspoon cream of tartar
1/4 cup Splenda® sweetener
1 teaspoon vanilla extract
1 teaspoon liquid Sweet'N Low® sweetener

Preheat oven to 375º. Spray a 9"x13" nonstick cake pan and then set aside. In a small bowl stir cocoa and instant coffee into boiling water until smooth. Place in refrigerator to cool. In a medium mixing bowl cream shake mix and butter together until thoroughly combined and not crumbly. Press dough evenly onto the bottom of prepared pan. Use thumb side of hand to press dough, not fingers. Bake 8 minutes. While crust is baking whip egg whites, cream of tartar, vanilla extract, and Sweet'N Low® with an electric mixer until foamy. Gradually whip in Splenda® 1 tablespoon at a time and continue whipping until very stiff and slightly shiny. Gently fold cooled cocoa mixture into egg whites, being careful not to deflate whites. Spread evenly on crust and return to oven for 15 minutes. Cool in pan on a rack. Cut into 32 equal pieces. Store covered in the refrigerator. Best when served cold.

32 Servings at 1.1 grams carbs each

Rhubarb Meringue Bars

A favorite at our house among family and friends

Crust:
1 1/2 cups plus 3 tablespoons Carb Solutions® vanilla shake mix
3/4 cup butter, softened (1 1/2 sticks)

Preheat oven to 350º. Butter and spray a 9"x13" nonstick cake pan and then set aside. In a medium mixing bowl cream together butter and shake mix until thoroughly combined. Press dough evenly onto the bottom of prepared pan using the thumb side of hand, not fingers. Bake 12 minutes or until lightly browned. Remove from oven and cool on a rack.

Filling:
2 cups fresh rhubarb, diced small (if using frozen use unsweetened
    rhubarb, do not thaw)
2/3 cup Splenda® sweetener
4 large egg yolks (reserve whites for meringue)
2/3 cup heavy whipping cream
1/2 teaspoon ground cinnamon
1/2 teaspoon guar gum

In a medium saucepan combine all filling ingredients except guar gum. Cook over medium heat stirring constantly until thickened. Reduce heat to low and continue to cook another 10-15 minutes, stirring occasionally until rhubarb is almost tender. Sprinkle guar gum over and stir in. Continue to cook for 3-4 minutes. When rhubarb has been cooking about 5 minutes make meringue.

Meringue:
4 large egg whites
1/2 teaspoon cream of tartar
1 teaspoon vanilla extract
4 tablespoons Splenda® sweetener

In a large mixing bowl whip egg whites, cream of tartar, and extract with an electric mixer until frothy. Gradually whip in Splenda® 1 tablespoon at a time. Continue to whip until very stiff and slightly shiny and then set aside. Increase oven temperature to 375º.

To Assemble:
Spread filling evenly over crust. Top with meringue, spreading evenly but making attractive swirls in meringue. Bake about 15 minutes or until meringue is nicely browned. Cool in pan on a rack. Cut into 12 equal pieces. Store covered in the refrigerator.

12 Servings at 4.5 grams carbs each

Sour Cream Nut Bars
Unbelievably good – no one could ever guess these are low carb

Crust:
1 - recipe Vanilla Cookie Crust (page 92) dough, do not bake

Preheat oven to 350°. Spray an 8" square nonstick cake pan. Press dough evenly onto bottom of pan using the thumb side of your hand, not fingers. Bake for 12 minutes and then cool in pan on a rack. While crust is cooling prepare topping.

Topping:
3/4 cup sour cream (1 gram carbs per 2 tablespoons)
1/2 cup Splenda® sweetener
1 1/2 teaspoons liquid Sweet'N Low® sweetener
1 large egg yolk
1/2 teaspoon guar gum
1 teaspoon vanilla extract
3/4 cup walnuts or pecans, toasted and chopped small

In a small saucepan whisk together first 5 ingredients until smooth. Cook over medium heat whisking constantly until thickened, about 4-5 minutes. Stir in vanilla extract and pour evenly over cooled crust. Top evenly with nuts and then bake for another 15-18 minutes. Cool in pan on a rack. When cool cut into 16 equal pieces. Store covered in the refrigerator.

16 Servings at 2.8 grams carbs each

Strawberry Cream Cheese Squares

Light and refreshing. Especially good after a heavy meal and oh so easy

2   teaspoons sugar-free strawberry Jell-O® powder
1/3   cup boiling water
1/4   cup cold water
1   cup fresh strawberries, hulled and sliced
8   oz. cream cheese, softened
2/3   cup heavy whipping cream
3   tablespoons Splenda® sweetener
1/2   teaspoon liquid Sweet'N Low® sweetener
1/2   teaspoon vanilla extract

Spray a 7"x11" pan with sides and then set aside. In a small bowl dissolve Jell-O® in boiling water stirring until completely dissolved. Stir in cold water and then refrigerate until syrupy. In a medium mixing bowl beat cream cheese with an electric mixer until smooth and fluffy. Add cream, sweeteners, and extract and beat until thick and smooth. Spread evenly in prepared pan and then refrigerate until Jell-O® is syrupy. When Jell-O® is ready, place sliced strawberries evenly over cream cheese layer in an attractive fashion. Carefully pour Jell-O® evenly over strawberries. Chill until set. Cut into 8 equal pieces. Store covered in the refrigerator.

8 Servings at 2.9 grams carbs each

Strawberry Ice Cream
Fresh berries give this a terrific homemade taste

2 cups heavy whipping cream
1 cup water
1 tablespoon sugar-free Jell-O® instant vanilla pudding mix
1/3 cup plus 2 teaspoons Splenda® sweetener
1 teaspoon vanilla extract
1 teaspoon strawberry extract
1 1/2 cups fresh strawberries, washed, hulled and chopped

In a medium mixing bowl whisk all ingredients except strawberries until well combined. Stir in berries. Pour into freezer bowl of electric ice cream maker while running. Mixture will be soft serve texture in about 20 minutes. Divide evenly into 10 small paper cups. Place a wooden stick into each if desired. Freeze until solid then store in a lock top bag. When ready to serve, warm the outside of the cup with your hands for about 15 seconds and then peel off the cup. You can also let set out until beginning to soften or soften in the microwave for about 15-30 seconds.

Note: If you do not have an ice cream maker you can pour the mixture into a pan and freeze it until it starts to crystallize. Remove from freezer and whip with an electric mixer for 1 minute. Pour evenly into 10 small cups and freeze as directed above.

10 Servings at 3.5 grams carbs each

Strawberry Layered Lemon Cheesecake

So delicious for company and yet easy enough to make anytime

1 small package sugar-free lemon Jell-O®, divided
1/3 cup boiling water
2 – 8 oz. packages cream cheese softened, divided
3 tablespoons Atkins® bake mix
1/2 teaspoon lemon zest, grated (yellow part only)
1/4 cup Splenda® sweetener
Pinch salt
2 large eggs
1 cup fresh strawberries, hulled and sliced
1 teaspoon liquid Sweet'N Low® sweetener
2/3 cup heavy whipping cream

Preheat oven to 325°. Spray a 7" or 7 1/2" springform pan and cover outside bottom and up sides with aluminum foil. In a small bowl dissolve 2 1/2 teaspoons Jell-O® in boiling water. Stir until dissolved, may take a few minutes, and then set aside. In a medium mixing bowl whip cream cheese with an electric mixer until soft and fluffy. Slowly beat in dissolved Jell-O® until smooth. Add bake mix, lemon zest, Splenda®, and salt. Whip until smooth. Add eggs and mix on low speed until eggs are just incorporated. Pour into prepared pan and rap several times on countertop to level. Bake for 30-35 minutes or until set. Cool completely in pan on a rack. While bottom layer is baking, mix strawberries with Sweet'N Low® sweetener and then set aside. When bottom layer is completely cool, top evenly with strawberries. In a small mixing bowl whip cream to soft peaks with an electric mixer and then set aside. In a medium mixing bowl whip remaining package cream cheese until very soft and fluffy. Add remaining dry Jell-O® and whipped cream and whip for about 30 seconds. Spread evenly over strawberry layer then chill for at least 4 hours. Cut into 8 equal pieces. Store covered in the refrigerator.

8 Servings at 5 grams carbs each

Sweet Roasted Nuts

These are so good you can't believe they are low carb

1 1/2 cups nuts, any kind (pecans or almonds are both good)
1 tablespoon butter
4 teaspoons Splenda® sweetener
Popcorn salt to taste

Preheat oven to 350°. Line a large baking pan with aluminum foil and then set aside. In a medium bowl melt butter in the microwave 30-40 seconds.

Add nuts, Splenda®, and popcorn salt and stir until combined. Transfer to prepared pan and spread evenly. Bake for 5 or 6 minutes, stir well and continue to bake another 5 or 6 minutes. Watch closely so they don't burn or get too dark. Cool to room temperature. Store in a tightly closed container.

6 – 1/4 cup Servings at 5.3 grams carbs each

Vanilla Ice Cream Patties

Wonderful little snack when you just want something small but satisfying and so easy to make

8 oz. cream cheese, softened
1 cup heavy whipping cream, whipped until thick but not stiff
3/4 teaspoon liquid Sweet'N Low® sweetener
1 teaspoon vanilla extract
1 tablespoon Carb Solutions® vanilla shake mix
1/4 cup plus 2 tablespoons Splenda® sweetener

Line a large baking sheet with waxed paper and then set aside. In a medium mixing bowl whip cream cheese with an electric mixer until soft and fluffy. Add remaining ingredients and whip until very thick. Place mixture in a pastry bag with a large round tip and pipe into 36 patties on prepared pan. You may also just drop them from a teaspoon and spread into patties. Place in freezer until hard and then peel off waxed paper and store in a covered container in the freezer.

36 patties at .6 grams carbs each

Maple Walnut Ice Cream Patties

The combination of these two makes this a real treat to have on hand

Replace vanilla extract with 1 tablespoon maple flavoring and add 4 tablespoons walnuts, toasted and finely chopped. Follow above directions.

40 patties at .7 grams carbs each

Mint Ice Cream Patties

The mint flavor is so refreshing in these little darlings

Replace vanilla extract with 1/2 teaspoon mint extract and add a few drops green food color. Follow above directions.

36 patties at .6 grams carbs each

Chocolate Fudge Sauce

Smooth and velvety - it's great on just about anything

1 cup heavy whipping cream
1 – 1 oz. square unsweetened baking chocolate, broken up
3/4 teaspoon liquid Sweet'N Low® sweetener
1 tablespoon unsweetened baking cocoa
1/4 cup plus 1 tablespoon Splenda® sweetener
Pinch of salt

In a small saucepan warm cream over low heat. While cream is heating melt chocolate in the microwave in a small bowl for 1 minute, stopping at 30 seconds to stir. If not melted after stirring well microwave at 15 second intervals, stirring after each until melted. Whisk chocolate and remaining ingredients into warm cream until well combined. Cook over low heat 15 minutes stirring frequently. Makes about 1 1/4 cups. Store covered in the refrigerator.

10 – 2 tablespoon Servings at 2.5 grams carbs each

Vanilla Sauce

Wonderful on bread pudding, strawberries or great on unfrosted cake

1 cup heavy whipping cream, divided
2 large egg yolks, beaten with a fork
2 tablespoons Splenda® sweetener
3/4 teaspoon liquid Sweet'N Low® sweetener
1 teaspoon vanilla extract

In a small saucepan whisk together 1/2 cup cream, egg yolks, and sweeteners. Cook over very low heat just until thickened, whisking constantly. Remove from heat and pour into a plastic bowl to cool. When cool place in refrigerator until cold. Do not cook too long or over too high heat or mixture will curdle and separate. If it does separate, whisk it in the plastic bowl until it gets creamy, then refrigerate until cold. In a medium bowl whip remaining 1/2 cup of cream and extract until thick but not stiff. Fold whipped cream into cold custard mixture. Serve immediately or refrigerate until serving time. Makes about 21 tablespoons.

21 - 1 tablespoon Servings at .5 grams carbs each

(AKES & FROSTINGS

Almond Crème Torte

This is a yummy dessert – the cake is very light with a fine texture making it a terrific choice for any occasion

Cake Layer:

5 large eggs, separated
1/2 teaspoon cream of tartar
3/4 cup blanched almond flour
2 teaspoons baking powder
3/4 cup Splenda® sweetener, divided (remove 2 tablespoons and set aside)
1 cup heavy whipping cream
1 teaspoon almond extract
1/4 cup sliced almonds

Preheat oven to 350°. Butter and spray 2 – 8" round nonstick cake pans and then set aside. In a large mixing bowl place egg whites and cream of tartar and then set aside. In a medium bowl whisk almond flour, baking powder, and Splenda® until blended. Whisk in egg yolks, cream, and almond extract until smooth and then set aside. Whip egg whites with an electric mixer until stiff but not dry. Gently fold egg yolk mixture into egg whites taking care not to deflate whites. Divide evenly into prepared pans. Rap on countertop to level. Sprinkle each with 1/2 of the almonds and 1 tablespoon of the reserved Splenda®. Bake for approximately 30-35 minutes or until golden brown and springs back when lightly touched with a finger. Cool in pans on racks for 5 minutes, then invert on cooling racks and cool to room temperature.

Filling:

1 cup heavy whipping cream
1/4 cup Splenda® sweetener
1/2 teaspoon almond extract
1/4 cup toasted almond flour (toast in a dry skillet over medium heat until lightly browned, stirring constantly and then cool)
1 tablespoon sugar-free Jell-O® instant vanilla pudding mix

In a medium bowl whip all filling ingredients with an electric mixer until stiff. Do not over beat or it will turn to butter. Place one layer almond side up on a cake plate. Spread with about 2/3 of the filling. Carefully place the second layer almond side up over the bottom layer. Garnish the top with remaining filling. Cut into 10 equal pieces. Store covered in the refrigerator.

10 Servings at 7 grams carbs each

Banana Flips

These will remind you of the Banana Flips that were
sold commercially except these are even better!

Pancakes:
2 large eggs, separated
1/4 teaspoon cream of tartar
1/2 cup heavy whipping cream
1/4 cup water
1 tablespoon baking powder
1 tablespoon vanilla extract
2 tablespoons butter, melted and cooled
2/3 cup Carb Solutions® vanilla shake mix
Dash of salt

In a medium mixing bowl place egg whites and cream of tartar and then set
aside. In another medium bowl whisk together remaining ingredients including
egg yolks. Whip egg whites with an electric mixer until stiff but not dry. Gently
fold egg yolk mixture into egg whites being careful not to deflate whites. Heat a
large nonstick griddle or skillet over medium heat. Wipe griddle with an oiled
paper towel. When a drop of water skitters on the griddle it is hot enough. Drop
batter by 1/4 cupfuls onto hot griddle spreading in a circle if necessary and then
cook until top begins to look dry. Turn and cook until other side is browned.
Cool on racks for 3 minutes then roll up and finish cooling on racks to room
temperature.

Banana Filling:
1 cup heavy whipping cream
1 tablespoon sugar-free Jell-O® instant banana cream pudding mix
1/4 teaspoon liquid Sweet'N Low® sweetener
2 tablespoons Splenda® sweetener

In a medium bowl whip all ingredients with an electric mixer until stiff. Do not
overbeat or it will turn to butter. Unroll each cooled pancake and spread 2 1/2
tablespoons filling onto 1/2 of each round. Fold in half and store covered in the
refrigerator. Makes 10 Banana Flips.

10 Servings at 2.5 grams carbs each

Blueberry Streusel Coffeecake

**This is great with coffee for breakfast or any time of the day.
I'm sure you'll enjoy this delight!**

Streusel:

2/3 cup Carb Solutions® vanilla shake mix
4 tablespoons butter, softened (1/2 stick)
1 teaspoon ground cinnamon
3 tablespoons walnuts or pecans, toasted and chopped small

In a small bowl stir all streusel ingredients together until well combined and crumbly and then set aside.

Cake:

4 tablespoons butter, softened (1/2 stick)
2/3 cup Splenda® sweetener
5 large eggs
3/4 cup blanched almond flour
2 teaspoons baking powder
1/4 cup heavy whipping cream
1 teaspoon vanilla extract
3/4 cup blueberries, fresh or frozen, unsweetened. If using frozen, do
   not thaw

Preheat oven to 350°. Spray an 8" square nonstick cake pan and then set aside. In a large mixing bowl cream together butter and Splenda®. Add eggs and beat with an electric mixer until well blended. In a small bowl mix almond flour and baking powder together. Add 1/2 of the almond flour to the egg mixture and beat until incorporated. Add 1/2 of cream to egg mixture and beat well. Add remaining almond flour and beat, then remaining cream and vanilla extract and beat well. Pour batter into prepared pan, top evenly with blueberries and then streusel. Bake for about 40 minutes or until springs back when lightly touched with a finger. Cut into 12 equal pieces. Store covered in the refrigerator.

12 Servings at 5.3 grams carbs each

Chocolate Fudge Cake

A chocolate lovers dream that is a very chocolaty, heavy
and dense cake. It's simply delicious!

1 oz. square unsweetened baking chocolate
6 large eggs, separated
1/2 teaspoon cream of tartar
3/4 cup Splenda® sweetener
2/3 cup Carb Solutions® chocolate shake mix
2 tablespoons unsweetened baking cocoa
1 cup heavy whipping cream
1 1/2 teaspoons vanilla extract

Preheat oven to 350°. In a small glass bowl or custard cup melt chocolate in the microwave until just melted, stopping and stirring every 30 seconds then set aside to cool. Butter and spray a deep 8" round cake pan; I also line the bottom with parchment and then set aside. In a large mixing bowl place egg whites and cream of tartar and then set aside. In a medium mixing bowl whisk together Splenda®, shake mix, and cocoa. Whisk in egg yolks, cream, and melted chocolate until well blended and then set aside. Whip egg whites with an electric mixer until stiff but not dry. Gently fold 1/2 of egg whites into chocolate mixture. Then fold remaining egg whites into mixture being careful not to deflate whites. Pour into prepared pan and smooth top evenly. Bake 35-40 minutes or until springs back when lightly touched with a finger. Cool on a rack for 10 minutes, then invert onto another rack to finish cooling. You may also leave in the pan if desired, just let cool completely on the rack. Cut into10 equal pieces. Store covered in the refrigerator. Best when served cold.

Note: If you are in a hurry and want a quick chocolate frosting, frost with
sugar-free Chocolate Twist® spread. Just be sure to count the carbs for the
amount you use.

Frosted Cake:

Peanut Butter Frosting (page 53), 7.2 grams carbs each serving

White Chocolate Mousse Frosting (page 53), 6.8 grams carbs each serving

Maple Cream Frosting (page 52), 5.8 grams carbs each serving

10 Servings at 5.2 grams carbs each (cake only)

Fresh Rhubarb Walnut Cake With Cream Cheese Frosting

You'll fall in love with this wonderful cake. Each bite will delight and tantalize your taste buds!

5 large eggs, separated
1/2 teaspoon cream of tartar
2 cups fresh rhubarb, diced small (do not use frozen, it will not work in this recipe)
1 cup heavy whipping cream
2/3 cup Splenda® sweetener
1 teaspoon ground cinnamon
1 1/2 teaspoons vanilla extract
1/3 cup Carb Solutions® vanilla shake mix
1 teaspoon xanthan gum
3 tablespoons walnuts, toasted and chopped fine
1 - recipe Cream Cheese Frosting (page 52)

Preheat oven to 350º. Butter and spray the sides of a <u>deep</u> 8" round nonstick cake pan. Line the bottom with baking parchment and then set aside. You can butter and spray the bottom if you wish instead of using parchment but you risk the cake sticking to the bottom. In a large mixing bowl place egg whites and cream of tartar and then set aside. In a medium bowl whisk remaining ingredients (except frosting), until well blended and then set aside. Whip egg whites with an electric mixer until stiff but not dry. Gently fold the rhubarb mixture into the egg whites being careful not to deflate whites. Pour into prepared pan and smooth top. Pan will be almost full. Bake for about 40-45 minutes or until firm to the touch and lightly browned. Cool in pan on a rack. When completely cooled, frost evenly with Cream Cheese Frosting. Cut into 10 equal pieces. Store covered in the refrigerator.

10 Servings at 6.4 grams carbs each

German Pineapple Küchen

You don't have to be German to enjoy this irresistible coffeecake. This one never lasts around our home!

Pineapple Spread:

1/4 cup plus 2 tablespoons low carb pineapple fruit spread (1
      tablespoon /2 grams carbs)
3 tablespoons Brown Sugar Twin® sweetener
4 tablespoons butter, melted and cooled
1 teaspoon ground cinnamon

In a small bowl mix fruit spread, sweetener, and butter and then set aside. Heavily butter a heavy nonstick ovenproof skillet and then spray. Spread fruit mixture evenly in the bottom of prepared skillet, sprinkle with cinnamon and then set aside.

Coffeecake:

6 large eggs, separated
2 large egg yolks (save these egg whites for an omelet or meringue)
1/2 teaspoon cream of tartar
1 cup heavy whipping cream
1 tablespoon vanilla extract
1/3 cup plus 3 tablespoons Carb Solutions® vanilla shake mix
2/3 cup Splenda® sweetener

Preheat oven to 350°. In a large mixing bowl place egg whites and cream of tartar and then set aside. In another large bowl whisk 8 egg yolks, cream, and vanilla extract until well blended. Whisk in shake mix and Splenda® until mixture is smooth and then set aside. Whip egg whites from 6 separated eggs with an electric mixer until stiff but not dry. Carefully fold yolk mixture into egg whites being careful not to deflate whites. Spread carefully over fruit layer in prepared pan. Bake for about 25-35 minutes or until springs back when lightly touched with a finger and is lightly browned. Cool in pan 7 minutes then run a spatula around sides to loosen. Place a large cake plate on top of pan right side down then quickly turn upside down holding plate and pan together tightly. Carefully remove pan. If any fruit mixture sticks to the pan, scrape it out and spread evenly over cake. Serve at room temperature or chilled. Cut into 12 equal pieces. Store covered in the refrigerator.

12 Servings at 4.3 grams carbs each

Merry Christmas Cake

Tastes great and looks beautiful. A wonderful dessert to put the finishing touch on your Holiday dinner

"Jewels":

1 small box sugar-free cherry Jell-O®
1 small box sugar-free lime Jell-O®

Prepare each box of Jell-O® separately as directed on box except using 3/4 cup cold water each instead of the usual full cup. Pour each flavor into a separate sprayed 9"x13" cake pan and chill until set. These will be a very thin layers. Prepare cake while these set up.

Cake:

5 large eggs, separated
1/2 teaspoon cream of tartar
3/4 cup blanched almond flour
2 teaspoons baking powder
1/4 teaspoon unsweetened cherry drink mix such as Kool-Aid® (0 carbs)
3/4 cup Splenda® sweetener
1 cup heavy whipping cream

Preheat oven to 350°. Butter and spray the sides of 2 – 8" round nonstick cake pans. Line the bottoms with baking parchment and then set aside. In a large mixing bowl place egg whites and cream of tartar and then set aside. In a medium mixing bowl whisk almond flour, baking powder, drink mix, and Splenda® until blended. Whisk in egg yolks and cream until smooth and then set aside. Whip egg whites with an electric mixer until stiff but not dry. Gently fold egg yolk mixture into egg whites taking care not to deflate whites. Divide evenly into prepared pans. Rap on counter to level. Bake 30-35 minutes or until springs back when lightly touched with a finger. Cool in pans 5 minutes then invert onto cooling racks and cool to room temperature.

Continued on next page.

Frosting:

2 cups heavy whipping cream
1 teaspoon vanilla extract
1 teaspoon sugar-free Jell-O® instant vanilla pudding mix
1/4 cup Splenda® sweetener
1/2 teaspoon liquid Sweet'N Low® sweetener

In a large bowl whip all ingredients with an electric mixer until stiff. Cover and keep refrigerated until needed.

Assembly:

Remove pans of firm Jell-O® one at a time from the refrigerator, lime flavor first. If you really want your cake to be extra special (remember this is for Christmas) take the tip of a knife and from one end of the pan, cut out 3 holly shaped leaves and place carefully on sprayed waxed paper then refrigerate. With the tip of your knife cut remaining Jell-O® into tiny cubes, just cut narrow strips in one direction then do the same in the other direction. You do not have to be perfect here, you just want little "jewels". Scrape from pan into a small bowl and refrigerate. Do the same thing with the cherry Jell-O® except cut three round circles for holly berries from one end of pan and refrigerate same as the leaves. Do the same with remaining cherry Jell-O® as with the lime flavor. A few hours before serving time place one cake layer upside down on a cake plate. Remove frosting and Jell-O® cubes from the refrigerator. Fold 2/3 cup of each flavor into the frosting. Spread about 2/3 cup frosting on first layer. Place top layer right side up carefully on bottom layer, lining up evenly. Frost the sides and then the top with remaining frosting. If you are using the holly decoration, remove from refrigerator and carefully place the leaves fanned out as holly, then place the red berries in a cluster where the ends of the leaves meet. Refrigerate up to 4 hours. Cut into 10 equal pieces. Store covered in the refrigerator.

10 Servings at 6.4 carbs each

Pumpkin Spice Cake

**Just the aroma of this delightful cake is heavenly —
great with cream cheese frosting or even a little whipped cream.
Oh so yummy!**

5 large eggs, separated
1/2 teaspoon cream of tartar
3/4 cup blanched almond flour
2 teaspoons baking powder
1/2 cup Splenda® sweetener
2 teaspoons ground cinnamon
1/4 teaspoon ground cloves
1/2 teaspoon ground ginger
1/4 cup walnuts, toasted and chopped small
1 1/2 teaspoons liquid Sweet'N Low® sweetener
1/2 cup canned solid pack pumpkin
1/2 cup heavy whipping cream
1 - recipe Cream Cheese Frosting (page 52)

Preheat oven to 350°. Butter and spray an 8" square nonstick cake pan and then set aside. In a large mixing bowl place egg whites and cream of tartar and then set aside. In a medium bowl whisk dry ingredients together. In a small bowl or measuring cup whisk egg yolks, liquid Sweet'N Low®, pumpkin, and cream until blended. Whisk into dry ingredients until well combined and then set aside. Whip egg whites with an electric mixer until stiff but not dry. Gently fold pumpkin mixture into egg whites being careful not to deflate whites. Pour into prepared pan, smooth top and bake for 25-35 minutes or until springs back when lightly touched with a finger. Cool in pan on a rack. When completely cool, frost evenly with Cream Cheese Frosting. Cut into 9 equal pieces. Store covered in the refrigerator.

9 Servings at 8.8 grams carbs each

Sour Cream Apple Spice Cake

This contains a small amount of apples
but what a scrumptious BIG apple flavor

5   large eggs, separated
1/2   teaspoon cream of tartar
1/2   cup butter, softened, divided
2/3   cup Splenda® sweetener
1/3   cup Carb Solutions® vanilla shake mix
1/3   cup heavy whipping cream
1/3   cup sour cream
2   teaspoons baking powder
1 1/2   teaspoons apple pie spice
1   tablespoon sugar-free Jell-O® instant butterscotch pudding mix
2   tablespoons Brown Sugar Twin® sweetener
1/4   cup walnuts, toasted and chopped small
1/2   of a 2 3/4" cooking apple peeled, cored, and sliced into thin
      crescents

Preheat oven to 350°. Spray an 8" round or square nonstick cake pan and then
set aside. In a large bowl place egg whites and cream of tartar and then set
aside. In a medium bowl whisk together egg yolks, 1/4 cup butter, Splenda®,
shake mix, cream, sour cream, baking powder, and apple pie spice until well
combined and then set aside. Place remaining 1/4 cup butter in the cake pan and
place in the oven just until melted, 2-4 minutes. Remove from oven and swirl
butter to evenly cover bottom of pan. Sprinkle pudding mix, Brown Sugar
Twin®, and walnuts evenly over butter. Lay apple slices evenly over walnuts in a
decorative fashion and then set aside. Whip egg whites with an electric mixer
until stiff but not dry. Gently fold yolk mixture into egg whites being careful not
to deflate whites. Scrape into prepared pan and smooth top. Bake about 40
minutes or until springs back when lightly touched with a finger. Cool 10
minutes in pan on a rack then cover with a cake plate. Carefully invert onto
plate. Cool to room temperature on plate on a rack. Cut into 12 equal pieces.
Store covered in the refrigerator.

12 Servings at 4.6 grams carbs each

Tiramisu

Although the ingredients in this fabulous dessert are
not traditional it is so excellent that one of my tasters says
it's the best she has ever tasted!

Cake:

5 large eggs, separated
1/2 teaspoon cream of tartar
3/4 cup toasted hazelnut flour
2 teaspoons baking powder
1/2 cup plus 2 tablespoons Splenda® sweetener
1 cup heavy whipping cream
1 teaspoon vanilla extract

Preheat oven to 350°. Butter sides of 2 - 8" round or square cake pans. Line
bottoms with baking parchment or waxed paper. If using waxed paper butter
paper and then set aside. In a large mixing bowl place egg whites and cream of
tartar and then set aside. In a small bowl whisk together hazelnut flour, baking
powder, and Splenda® and then set aside. In a medium bowl whisk egg yolks,
cream, and vanilla extract until combined. Whisk into dry ingredients until
smooth. Whip egg whites with an electric mixer until stiff but not dry. Gently
fold hazelnut flour mixture into egg whites being careful not to deflate whites.
Divide batter evenly between prepared pans and rap gently on countertop to
release air bubbles. Bake for 30-35 minutes or until springs back when lightly
touched with a finger. Cool in pans on racks for 10 minutes then carefully
remove from pans and finished cooling on racks to room temperature. Cover
and chill until cold. You will have 2 thin layers.

Chocolate Ganache Filling:

1/2 cup plus 2 tablespoons heavy whipping cream
2 tablespoons Splenda® sweetener
1/2 – 1 oz. square unsweetened baking chocolate, chopped
3 tablespoons sugar-free Chocolate Hazelnut Twist® spread

In a small saucepan heat cream and Splenda® over medium heat to boiling. Stir
in baking chocolate, remove from heat and let set for 5 minutes. Whisk in
Twist® spread until mixture is smooth. Transfer to a plastic bowl and refrigerate
until thick enough to spread.

Continued on next page.

Mocha Cream:

1   teaspoon instant coffee, dissolved in 2 teaspoons boiling water and
     then cooled
1   cup heavy whipping cream
1 1/2   teaspoons sugar-free Jell-O® instant chocolate fudge or chocolate
     pudding mix
2   tablespoons Splenda® sweetener
Chocolate Drizzle (page 19)

In a medium mixing bowl whip all ingredients except Chocolate Drizzle with an
electric mixer until very thick. Cover and refrigerate until you are ready to
assemble the Tiramisu.

To Assemble:

Carefully slice each chilled cake layer into 2 very thin layers. These will be so
thin you can almost see through them. Spread a small amount of Mocha Cream
on the cut sides then put split layers back together. You will then have 2 double
layers. Place one double layer onto cake plate bottom side up. Carefully spread
Chocolate Ganache evenly over top. Place remaining double layer carefully on
top, right side up. Frost cake with remaining Mocha Cream then top with
Chocolate Drizzle. Cut into 12 equal pieces. Store covered in the refrigerator.

12 Servings at 5.4 grams carbs each

Cream Cheese Frosting

4 oz. cream cheese, softened (1/2 – 8 oz. bar)
3 tablespoons butter, softened
1 teaspoon vanilla extract
1/2 cup heavy whipping cream
1/4 cup Splenda® sweetener
1 1/2 teaspoons sugar-free Jell-O® instant vanilla pudding mix

In a medium bowl whip cream cheese and butter with an electric mixer until fluffy. Add remaining ingredients and whip until thick. Spread on cooled dessert. Store covered in the refrigerator.

Whole recipe is 14.5 grams carbs

Maple Cream Frosting

2/3 cup heavy whipping cream
2 teaspoons sugar-free Jell-O® instant butterscotch pudding mix
1 teaspoon maple flavoring
1 1/2 teaspoons liquid Sweet'N Low® sweetener

In a medium bowl whip all ingredients with an electric mixer until thick. Spread on cooled dessert. Store covered in the refrigerator.

Whole recipe is 6 grams carbs

Peanut Butter Frosting

3　tablespoons peanut butter (6 grams carbs per 2 tablespoons)
4　tablespoons butter, softened (1/2 stick)
1　teaspoon vanilla extract
1/2　cup heavy whipping cream
1/4　cup Splenda® sweetener
2　teaspoons sugar-free Jell-O® instant butterscotch pudding mix

In a medium bowl whip peanut butter and butter with an electric mixer until smooth. Add remaining ingredients and whip until thick. Spread on cooled dessert. Store covered in the refrigerator.

Whole recipe is 20.2 grams carbs

White Chocolate Mousse Frosting

2　Ross® white delight candy bars, melted and cooled
4　tablespoons butter, softened (1/2 stick)
1　teaspoon vanilla extract
1/2　cup heavy whipping cream
3　tablespoons Splenda® sweetener
2　teaspoons sugar-free Jell-O® instant white chocolate pudding mix

In a medium bowl whip all ingredients with an electric mixer until thick. Spread on cooled dessert. Store covered in the refrigerator.

Whole recipe is 15.5 grams carbs

COOKIES

Almond Slices

Super simple and great to have in the refrigerator for fresh baked cookies at a moments notice

1 cup butter, softened (2 sticks)
2 cups Carb Solutions® vanilla shake mix
1/4 cup blanched almond flour
1/2 cup Splenda® sweetener
1 large egg
1 teaspoon almond extract
1/4 cup sliced almonds

In a medium bowl cream together butter, shake mix, almond flour, and Splenda®. Stir in remaining ingredients and mix thoroughly. On a large piece of waxed paper or plastic wrap, form dough into a log about 10" long. Refrigerate at least several hours or until firm. Preheat oven to 375°. Slice into 1/4" slices and place on a sprayed cookie sheet. Bake for about 8-10 minutes or until lightly browned and set. Cool on a rack. Store covered in the refrigerator. Best when served cold.

36 Cookies at 1 gram carbs each

Banana Nut Logs

No monkey business here - these are great banana nut cookies!

1 cup butter, softened (2 sticks)
2 1/4 cups Carb Solutions® vanilla shake mix
1 tablespoon sugar-free Jell-O® instant banana cream pudding mix
1/4 cup Splenda® sweetener
1 large egg
2 tablespoons heavy whipping cream
1 teaspoon banana extract
1/4 cup walnuts, toasted and chopped small

Preheat oven to 375°. Spray a nonstick cookie sheet and then set aside. In a large bowl cream together first four ingredients. Stir in remaining ingredients until thoroughly mixed. Form into 36 balls and roll each between palms of hands into 2" logs. Shape each log into a crescent tapering ends like a banana. Place on prepared cookie sheet 2" apart. Bake for 10 minutes and then cool on a rack until completely cooled. Store covered in the refrigerator. Best when served cold.

36 Cookies at .8 grams carbs each

Chocolate Chunk Cookies

Have you missed chocolate chip cookies?
Well try these on for size!

1 cup butter, softened (2 sticks)
2 1/4 cups Carb Solutions® vanilla shake mix
3 tablespoons Brown Sugar Twin® sweetener
1 large egg
1 teaspoon baking powder
1 teaspoon vanilla extract
2 Ross® dark delight chocolate bars, chopped size of chocolate chips
1/4 cup walnuts, toasted and chopped small
Splenda® sweetener for flattening

Preheat oven to 350º. Spray a nonstick cookie sheet and then set aside. In a medium mixing bowl cream first 3 ingredients thoroughly. Stir in egg, baking powder, and vanilla extract and mix well. Stir in chopped chocolate and walnuts and mix until evenly distributed. Shape into 1" balls and place on prepared pan 1 1/2" apart. Flatten with the bottom of a sprayed glass dipped in Splenda® to about silver dollar size. Dip glass into Splenda® between cookies shaking off excess. Bake for 11-12 minutes or until lightly browned and set. Cool to room temperature on a rack. Store covered in the refrigerator. Best when served cold.

48 Cookies at .5 grams carbs each

Chocolate Filled Chocolate Thumbprints

You will LOVE these beautiful chocolate wonders. If you didn't know they were low carb you would never believe it.

1 cup butter, softened (2 sticks)
2 cups Carb Solutions® chocolate shake mix
2 large eggs
1 teaspoon vanilla extract
1/4 cup walnut meal (you can substitute pecan meal or almond meal if desired)
1/3 cup plus 2 tablespoons sugar-free Chocolate Twist® spread or you can substitute sugar-free Chocolate Hazelnut Twist®

Preheat oven to 375°. Spray a nonstick cookie sheet and then set aside. Place walnut meal in a small shallow dish and then set aside. In a medium bowl cream butter and shake mix until thoroughly combined. Add eggs and vanilla extract and mix well. Shape into 1" balls, roll in walnut meal and place on prepared pan 1 1/2" apart. Make a deep indentation in each cookie with thumb. Bake 10-11 minutes. Cool on racks to room temperature. Fill each indentation with 1/2 teaspoon Chocolate Twist® spread. Store covered in the refrigerator. The Chocolate Twist® spread will firm up in the refrigerator. Best when served cold.

Note: These are also great with Crunchy Peanut Butter filling (page 61). Increase the carbs to 1.3 grams each.

44 Cookies at .9 grams carbs each

Chocolate Walnut Refrigerator Cookies

It's hard to believe how easy these are to make.
They make a great chocolate treat and the dough keeps well in
the refrigerator so you can have fresh cookies anytime

1 cup butter, softened (2 sticks)
2 1/4 cups Carb Solutions® chocolate shake mix
2 tablespoons Splenda® sweetener
1 large egg
1/2 cup walnuts, toasted and chopped small

In a medium bowl cream butter, shake mix, and Splenda® thoroughly. Stir in egg and walnuts until well mixed and walnuts are evenly distributed. On a large piece of waxed paper or plastic wrap, form into a log about 10" long. Wrap tightly and refrigerate several hours or until firm. Refrigerated dough keeps well for days so you can bake them when you want. Preheat oven to 375°. With a sharp knife slice into 1/4" slices. Place on a sprayed nonstick cookie sheet 1 1/2" apart. Bake for 8-10 minutes or until set. Cool on a rack. Store covered in the refrigerator. Best when served cold.

40 Cookies at 1 gram carbs each

Cinnamon Cookies

These will melt in your mouth

1 cup butter, softened (2 sticks)
2 1/4 cups Carb Solutions® vanilla shake mix
1 tablespoon ground cinnamon, divided
4 tablespoons Brown Sugar Twin® sweetener, divided

Preheat oven to 375°. Spray a nonstick cookie sheet and then set aside. In a small bowl mix together 1 teaspoon cinnamon and 2 tablespoons Brown Sugar Twin® and then set aside. In a medium bowl combine remaining ingredients including remaining 2 teaspoons cinnamon and 2 tablespoons Brown Sugar Twin®. Roll into 1" balls, roll in reserved cinnamon and Brown Sugar Twin® mixture and place on prepared cookie sheet 1 1/2" apart. Flatten slightly with the bottom of a sprayed glass and bake 8-10 minutes or until lightly browned and set. Let cool on cookie sheet on a rack for 7 minutes. Then carefully remove to a rack to finish cooling. These are very delicate but firm up after refrigerating. Store covered in the refrigerator. Best when served cold.

40 Cookies at .7 grams carbs each

Crunchy Filled Peanut Butter Drops

These look as good as they taste and if you are a peanut butter lover you'll be on cloud nine

Cookies:

1/2 cup butter, softened (1 stick)
1/2 cup creamy peanut butter (6 grams carbs /2 tablespoons)
2 cups Carb Solutions® vanilla shake mix
2 tablespoons Splenda® sweetener
1 large egg
1 teaspoon vanilla extract

Preheat oven to 375°. Spray a nonstick cookie sheet and then set aside. In a medium bowl cream butter, peanut butter, shake mix, and Splenda® thoroughly. Add egg and mix well and then set aside.

Crunchy Filling:

1/4 cup plus 2 tablespoons chunky peanut butter
     (6 grams carbs/2 tablespoons)
2 tablespoons Splenda® sweetener
1 large egg white

In a small bowl mix filling ingredients thoroughly. Shape dough into 36 - 1" balls. Place on prepared cookie sheet 2" apart. Make a deep indentation in each cookie with thumb. Spoon 1/2 teaspoon filling into each indentation. Bake for 10-11 minutes. Cool in pan on rack for 10 minutes. Gently remove from pan and finish cooling on rack to room temperature. Store covered in the refrigerator. Best when served cold.

36 Servings at 2 grams carbs each

Fruit Filled Thumbprints

These little gems are so colorful, taste wonderful and look beautiful on a cookie tray. I like to use several different fruit flavors for color contrast

1 cup butter, softened (2 sticks)
2 cups Carb Solutions® vanilla shake mix
1 large egg
1/2 teaspoon vanilla extract
1/2 teaspoon almond extract
7 tablespoons low carb fruit spread, any flavor
   (2 grams carbs per 1 tablespoon)

Preheat oven to 375°. Spray a nonstick cookie sheet and then set aside. In a medium bowl cream butter and shake mix thoroughly. Add egg and extracts and mix well. Shape into 40 - 1" balls. If dough is too soft to work with refrigerate 30-40 minutes. Place each ball on prepared cookie sheet 1 1/2" apart. Make a deep indentation in each cookie with thumb. Fill each indentation with 1/2 teaspoon fruit spread. Bake about 10-12 minutes or until lightly browned and set. Cool on a rack to room temperature. Store covered in the refrigerator. Best when served cold.

40 Cookies at .7 grams carbs each

Jelly Bean Jewels

These low carb Jelly Beans are so good.
I never cared for Jelly Beans before but these are so yummy
and colorful in the cookies.

1 cup butter, softened (2 sticks)
2 tablespoons Brown Sugar Twin® sweetener
1 teaspoon vanilla extract
1/2 teaspoon almond extract
2 1/4 cups Carb Solutions® vanilla shake mix
1 large egg
1/2 cup Carbolite® sugar-free jelly beans, cut up with sprayed scissors
1/4 cup walnuts, toasted and chopped small
1/4 cup Splenda® sweetener

Preheat oven to 375°. Spray a nonstick cookie sheet and then set aside. In a medium bowl cream together butter, Brown Sugar Twin®, extracts, and shake mix until thoroughly mixed. Stir in egg until well combined. Stir in jelly beans and walnuts and mix until evenly distributed. Shape into 1" balls and place on prepared cookie sheet 1 1/2" apart. Place Splenda® in a small bowl. Flatten with the bottom of a sprayed glass dipped in Splenda®. Dip glass into Splenda® between cookies shaking off excess. Bake for about 10 minutes or until lightly browned and set. Cool on a rack. Store covered in the refrigerator. Best when served cold.

36 Cookies at .6 grams each

Maple Nut Cookies

You can use either walnuts or pecans in these or skip the nuts
if you don't care for them. Either way they are yummy.

1 cup butter, softened (2 sticks)
2/3 cup Carb Solutions® vanilla shake mix
1/2 cup Atkins® bake mix
1/3 cup Splenda® sweetener
1 teaspoon baking powder
1 large egg
1 1/2 tablespoons maple flavoring
1/3 cup walnuts or pecans, toasted and chopped small

Preheat oven to 350°. Spray a nonstick cookie sheet and then set aside. In a
medium bowl cream butter, shake mix, bake mix, Splenda®, and baking powder
thoroughly. Stir in egg, maple flavoring and nuts until well combined and nuts
are evenly distributed. Drop from teaspoon on prepared cookie sheet 1 1/2"
apart. Bake for 10-11 minutes or until lightly browned and set. Cool on a rack to
room temperature. Store covered in the refrigerator. Best when served cold.

40 Cookies at .5 grams carbs each

Minty Christmas Trees

I was so thrilled to be able to make this dough work
with a cookie press. They were such a wonderful addition
to my Christmas cookie tray

1 cup butter, softened (2 sticks)
2 1/4 cups Carb Solutions® vanilla shake mix
1 large egg
1 teaspoon mint extract
Few drops green food color (vary according to intensity you desire)

Preheat oven to 375°. In a medium bowl cream butter and shake mix thoroughly.
Stir in remaining ingredients until well mixed. Place dough in a cookie press
with the Christmas tree disc in place. Press trees onto ungreased cookie sheet as
directed by cookie press instructions. If you don't have a cookie press, shape
into small 1/2" balls and flatten slightly. Bake about 8-10 minutes or until
slightly browned and set. Cool on a rack to room temperature. Store covered in
the refrigerator. Best when served cold.

Approximately 70 cookies at .2 grams carbs each

Orange Dreams

A nice refreshing change of pace. Fresh orange zest really
gives these a flavor boost and the dough keeps well in the
refrigerator so fresh cookies are only minutes away

1 cup butter, softened (2 sticks)
2 1/4 cups Carb Solutions® vanilla shake mix
1/4 cup Splenda® sweetener
1 large egg
1 tablespoon orange zest, orange part only
1/2 teaspoon orange extract

In a medium bowl cream butter, shake mix, and Splenda®. Stir in remaining
ingredients until well mixed. On waxed paper or plastic wrap, form into a log
about 10" long. Wrap tightly and refrigerate at least several hours or until firm.
Preheat oven to 375°. Slice into 1/4" rounds and place on a sprayed nonstick
cookie sheet 1 1/2" apart. Bake for 8-10 minutes or until lightly browned. Cool
on a rack to room temperature. Store covered in the refrigerator. Best when
served cold.

36 Cookies at .6 grams carbs each

Peanut Butter Cookies

Amazingly these taste just like the peanut butter cookies
we grew up eating, but without the carbs.
I know you'll love them too!

1/2 cup butter, softened (1 stick)
1/2 cup creamy peanut butter (6 grams carbs per 2 tablespoons)
2 1/4 cups Carb Solutions® vanilla shake mix
2 large eggs
1 teaspoon vanilla extract
3 tablespoons Splenda® sweetener

Preheat oven to 375°. Spray a nonstick cookie sheet and then set aside. In a
medium bowl cream butter, peanut butter, and shake mix thoroughly. Add eggs
and vanilla extract and mix well. Shape into 1" balls and place on prepared
cookie sheet 1 1/2" apart. Place Splenda® in a small shallow bowl. Spray a fork
with cooking spray and then dip into Splenda®. Press each cookie with fork in
crisscross fashion, dipping fork in Splenda® between each cookie. Bake for
10-11 minutes or until lightly browned and set. Cool on a rack to room
temperature. Store covered in the refrigerator. Best when served cold.

36 Cookies at 1.1 grams carbs each

Pecan Refrigerator Cookies

If you like "Pecan Sandies" you will love these and it just doesn't get any easier than this

1 cup butter, softened (2 sticks)
2 1/4 cups Carb Solutions® vanilla shake mix
1/4 cup Brown Sugar Twin® sweetener
1 large egg
1/2 cup pecans, toasted and chopped small
2 teaspoons vanilla extract

In a medium bowl cream butter, shake mix, and Brown Sugar Twin® thoroughly. Stir in remaining ingredients until well mixed and pecans are evenly distributed. On a large piece of waxed paper or plastic wrap, form into a log about 11" long. Wrap tightly and refrigerate at least several hours or until firm. Refrigerated dough keeps well for days so you can bake them when you want. Preheat oven to 375°. With a sharp knife slice into 1/4" slices and place on a sprayed nonstick cookie sheet 1 1/2" apart. Bake for 8-10 minutes or until lightly browned and set. Cool on a rack to room temperature. Store covered in the refrigerator. Best when served cold.

40 Cookies at .8 grams each

Piña Colada Cookies

Like a tropical breeze these will delight your senses and taste buds

1 cup butter, softened (2 sticks)
2 1/4 cups Carb Solutions® vanilla shake mix
1/2 cup Splenda® sweetener
1 large egg
1 teaspoon baking powder
1/2 cup low carb pineapple fruit spread (2 grams carbs per
    1 tablespoon)
1 1/2 teaspoons coconut extract

Preheat oven to 350°. Spray a nonstick cookie sheet and then set aside. In a medium bowl cream butter, shake mix, and Splenda® thoroughly. Stir in remaining ingredients until well mixed. Drop from a teaspoon onto prepared cookie sheet 1 1/2" apart. Bake for 11-13 minutes or until lightly browned and set. Cool on rack to room temperature. Store covered in the refrigerator. Best when served cold.

36 Cookies at 1.2 grams carbs each

Russian Tea Cakes

Russian Tea Cakes have always been my husband's favorite cookie so you can imagine how thrilled he was when I developed this low carb version. My tasters really loved this one too!

Cookies:

1   cup butter, softened (2 sticks)
2   cups Carb Solutions® vanilla shake mix
1   tablespoon soy protein powder (0 carbs)
1/2 cup Splenda® sweetener
2   teaspoons vanilla extract
1/4 cup pecans, toasted and chopped fine

Preheat oven to 375°. In a medium bowl cream butter, shake mix, soy protein powder, and Splenda® thoroughly. Stir in vanilla extract and pecans until well mixed and pecans are evenly distributed. Shape into 40 – 1" balls and place on a nonstick cookie sheet 1 1/2" apart. Bake for 11-13 minutes or until lightly browned and set. While cookies are baking prepare coating. Cool on cookie sheet on a rack for 5-7 minutes. Carefully remove from sheet and continue to cool on rack.

Coating:

1/4 cup Splenda® sweetener
1/4 cup Carb Solutions® vanilla shake mix
2   tablespoons pecan meal, toasted

In a small shallow bowl mix all ingredients thoroughly. While cookies are still slightly warm carefully roll in coating, shaking off excess. These are quite delicate but will firm up a little when refrigerated. Cool to room temperature. Store covered in the refrigerator. Best when served cold.

40 Cookies at 1 gram carbs each

Spice Cookies

You can't believe there is no molasses in these cookies
because they sure taste like there is. They are a big hit
with my family and friends

- 1 cup butter, softened (2 sticks)
- 2 1/4 cups Carb Solutions® vanilla shake mix
- 1/2 cup Splenda® sweetener, divided
- 1/4 teaspoon plus 1/8 teaspoon ground cloves
- 1 teaspoon ground ginger
- 1 tablespoon ground cinnamon
- 1 large egg

Preheat oven to 375°. Spray a nonstick cookie sheet and then set aside. Place 1/4 cup Splenda® in a small shallow bowl and set aside. In a medium bowl cream butter, shake mix, remaining 1/4 cup Splenda®, and spices thoroughly. Stir in egg until well mixed. Shape into 1" balls and place on prepared cookie sheet 2" apart. Flatten with the bottom of a glass, sprayed and then dipped in Splenda®. Dip glass in Splenda® between each cookie, shaking off excess. Bake 8-10 minutes. Cool on a rack to room temperature. Store covered in the refrigerator. Best when served cold.

40 Cookies at .8 grams carbs each

"Sugar Cookies"

You'll find it hard to believe but these taste just like old-fashioned sugar cookies without a speck of sugar

1 cup butter, softened (2 sticks)
2 1/4 cups Carb Solutions® vanilla shake mix
1/2 cup Splenda® sweetener, divided
1/2 teaspoon vanilla extract
1 large egg

Preheat oven to 375°. Spray a nonstick cookie sheet and then set aside. Place 1/4 cup Splenda® in a small shallow bowl and then set aside. In a medium bowl cream butter, shake mix, remaining Splenda®, and vanilla extract thoroughly. Stir in egg until well mixed. Shape into 1" balls and place on prepared cookie sheet 2" apart. Flatten with the bottom of a glass, sprayed and then dipped in Splenda®. Dip glass in Splenda® between each cookie, shaking off excess. Bake 8-10 minutes. Cool on a rack to room temperature. Store covered in the refrigerator. Best when served cold.

40 Cookies at .7 grams carbs each

PIES & CRUSTS

Banana Peanut Butter Pie

Simply irresistible - banana and peanut butter flavors
just seem to go together.

1 – recipe Vanilla Cookie Crust (page 92) or
   Peanut Butter Crust (page 91)
Baked and cooled

Peanut Butter Topping:
1 tablespoon heavy whipping cream
2 tablespoons butter, softened
2 tablespoons chunky peanut butter (6 grams carbs per 2 tablespoons)
2 tablespoons Splenda® sweetener

In a small bowl mix above ingredients until well blended and then set aside.

Banana Filling:
2 cups heavy whipping cream
2 tablespoons sugar-free Jell-O® instant banana pudding mix
1 teaspoon banana extract
1/4 cup Splenda® sweetener
Chocolate Drizzle (page 19)

In a medium mixing bowl whip above ingredients, except Chocolate Drizzle,
until stiff. Pie will not cut nicely if not whipped stiff. Scrape into cooled crust
and spread evenly. Drop peanut butter topping by small spoonfuls randomly over
banana filling. Swirl into filling with a knife in an attractive fashion as evenly
as possible. Top with Chocolate Drizzle. Refrigerate at least 2 hours. Cut into 8
equal pieces. Store covered in the refrigerator.

8 Servings at 5.1 grams carbs each
with Vanilla Cookie Crust

8 Servings at 6.2 grams carbs each
with Peanut Butter Crust

Butterscotch Pecan Chiffon Pie

Light and so tasty with toasted pecans. Toasting the nuts makes such a big difference in flavor.

1 – recipe Vanilla Cookie Crust dough, (page 92) do not bake
2 tablespoons pecans, toasted and chopped small
1/2 teaspoon butterscotch or caramel extract

Preheat oven to 350°. Spray a 9" pie pan and then set aside. In a medium bowl mix above ingredients until well mixed and pecans are well distributed. Press dough evenly on bottom and up sides of prepared pan with the thumb side of hand. Bake 12 minutes and then cool in pan on a rack.

Filling:

2 cups heavy whipping cream
2 tablespoons sugar-free Jell-O® instant butterscotch pudding mix
1/2 teaspoon butterscotch or caramel extract
1/4 cup Brown Sugar Twin® sweetener
2 tablespoons pecans, toasted and chopped fine
Chocolate Drizzle, (page 19) optional

In a medium mixing bowl whip all filling ingredients except Chocolate Drizzle, if using, with an electric mixer until stiff. Pie will not cut nicely if not whipped stiff. Scrape into cooled crust and spread evenly. Top with Chocolate Drizzle if using. Refrigerate at least 2 hours. Cut into 8 equal pieces. Store covered in the refrigerator.

8 Servings at 4.4 grams carbs each

Cherry Cream Cheese Pie

Wonderful cheesecake pie with a delicious cookie crust.
Great company fare at only 6 grams of carbs per serving.

Cherry Layer:
2/3 cup canned unsweetened sour pie cherries packed in water,
      drained, reserving 1/2 cup liquid (NOT cherry pie filling)
1/2 cup Splenda® sweetener
1/4 teaspoon xanthan gum
1/4 teaspoon almond extract
6 drops red food color

In a small bowl combine Splenda® and xanthan gum and then set aside. In a
small nonstick saucepan mix reserved 1/2 cup cherry liquid and Splenda®
mixture. Cook over medium heat stirring constantly until thickened, should take
about 3-5 minutes. Remove from heat and stir in cherries, almond extract, and
food color. Pour into a plastic bowl to cool and then set aside.

Crust and Topping:
1 1/3 sticks butter, softened (1/2 cup plus 5 tablespoons & 1 teaspoon)
1 1/3 cups Carb Solutions® vanilla shake mix
1/2 teaspoon vanilla extract

Preheat oven to 375°. Spray a 9" pie pan and then set aside. In a medium bowl
cream together butter and shake mix thoroughly. Stir in vanilla extract until well
mixed. Remove 1/3 cup and refrigerate until needed. Press remaining dough on
the bottom and up the sides of prepared pan using thumb side of hand. Bake 7
minutes then cool on a rack. Reduce oven temp to 350°.

Continued on next page.

Cream Cheese Layer:

2 - 8 oz. packages cream cheese, softened
2 tablespoons heavy whipping cream
1 teaspoon vanilla extract
1/2 cup Splenda® sweetener
1 large egg

In a medium bowl beat cream cheese with an electric mixer until smooth and fluffy. Beat in cream and vanilla extract until smooth. Add Splenda® and beat until thoroughly mixed. Add egg and mix on low speed until just incorporated. Pour over partially baked crust and smooth top. Bake 20 minutes. Remove from oven and carefully spread cherry mixture evenly over top. Crumble reserved dough evenly over cherry layer. Bake another 15 minutes or until set. Cool to room temperature on a rack and then refrigerate until cold. Cut into 10 equal servings. Store covered in the refrigerator.

10 Servings at 6 grams carbs each

Fresh Strawberry Glaće Pie

What a treat this is and so beautiful too, especially when homegrown berries are available

1 - recipe Vanilla Cookie Crust, (page 92) baked and cooled

Filling:
4 cups fresh strawberries, washed, hulled, and dried with paper towels, then refrigerated until needed
1/2 teaspoon unsweetened strawberry drink mix, such as Kool-Aid® (0 carbs)
1/2 cup Splenda® sweetener
1/2 teaspoon xanthan gum
1/4 cup sugar-free strawberry syrup (0 carbs)
1/2 teaspoon strawberry extract
3/4 cup water

In a small saucepan whisk drink mix, Splenda®, and xanthan gum together. Whisk in syrup, strawberry extract, and water until well blended. Bring to a full boil over high heat, whisking constantly. Reduce heat to low and continue to cook for 4 minutes, whisking frequently. Remove from heat and transfer to a large plastic bowl. Refrigerate until cool. When cooled add strawberries and toss gently to coat. Arrange berries point up in an attractive fashion on crust. Drizzle any remaining glaze over berries. Prepare Sweetened Whipped Cream. Pipe on pie with a pastry bag and a star tip or serve each piece with a dollop of topping. Cut into 8 equal pieces. Refrigerate at least 2 hours. Store covered in the refrigerator.

8 Servings at 8.6 grams each

Sweetened Whipped Cream

Topping:
1 cup heavy whipping cream
1 1/2 teaspoons liquid Sweet'N Low® sweetener
1/2 teaspoon vanilla extract

In a small mixing bowl whip all topping ingredients with an electric mixer until thick.

6.6 grams carbs total

Grasshopper Pie

Among my recipe tasters, this was a top favorite with
low carbers and non low carbers alike. It not only looks beautiful
but also tastes wonderful and is so easy.

1 - recipe Chocolate Cookie Crust, (page 90) baked and cooled

Filling:
2 cups heavy whipping cream
2 tablespoons sugar-free Jell-O® instant white chocolate pudding mix
1/4 cup Splenda® sweetener
1 teaspoon mint extract
6 drops green food color
Chocolate Drizzle (page 19)

In a medium mixing bowl whip all filling ingredients except Chocolate Drizzle
with an electric mixer until stiff. Pie will not cut nicely if not whipped stiff.
Scrape into cooled crust and spread evenly. Top with Chocolate Drizzle.
Refrigerate at least 2 hours. Cut into 8 equal servings. Store covered in the
refrigerator.

8 Servings at 4.7 grams each

Maple Pecan Pie

I served this dessert to company, mostly non low carbers and they were crazy about it. It's great topped with sweetened whipped cream - just be sure to count the extra carbs

1 - recipe Vanilla Cookie Crust, (page 92) baked 10 minutes and cooled

Filling:
1 cup Splenda® sweetener
1 cup sugar-free maple syrup (0 carbs, be sure to read the label, some say sugar-free but have a lot of carbs)
2 tablespoons butter, softened
1 1/2 teaspoons liquid Sweet'N Low® sweetener
1 1/2 teaspoons vanilla extract
4 large eggs, lightly beaten
1 cup pecan halves

In a medium saucepan mix Splenda®, syrup, butter, and Sweet'N Low® until thoroughly combined. Bring to a boil over medium high heat, remove from heat, pour into a plastic bowl and cool until barely warm. You can speed this step up by placing in the refrigerator. Preheat oven to 350°. When syrup mixture is barely warm add eggs and vanilla extract and mix thoroughly. Sprinkle pecans evenly in the bottom of the crust. Pour filling carefully over pecans. Bake about 30 minutes or until set. Cool in pan on a rack. When completely cool, refrigerate at least 2 hours. Cut into 8 equal servings. Store covered in the refrigerator.

Note: Sweetened Whipped Cream (page 78). Make sure to count the added carbs.

8 Servings at 6.8 grams carbs each

Mocha Chiffon Pie

The hint of coffee flavor in this dessert makes it just right.
It's so good melded with the chocolate

1 - recipe Chocolate Cookie Crust, (page 90) baked and cooled

Filling:

2 teaspoons instant decaffeinated coffee dissolved in 1 tablespoon hot
water and then cooled
2 cups heavy whipping cream
3 tablespoons sugar-free Jell-O® instant chocolate fudge or chocolate
pudding mix
1 teaspoon liquid Sweet'N Low® sweetener
1 teaspoon vanilla extract
Chocolate Drizzle (page 19)

In a medium mixing bowl whip all filling ingredients except Chocolate Drizzle
with an electric mixer until stiff. Pie will not cut nicely if not whipped stiff.
Scrape into cooled crust and spread evenly. Top with Chocolate Drizzle.
Refrigerate at least 2 hours. Cut into 8 equal pieces. Store covered in the
refrigerator.

8 Servings at 3.9 grams each

Peanut Butter Fudge Pie

Rich and chocolaty – A wonderful peanut buttery combination that will delight your taste buds!

1 1/2 - 1 oz. squares unsweetened baking chocolate
1 cup butter (2 sticks)
5 large eggs
1 cup Splenda® sweetener
3 tablespoons almond flour
1 teaspoon baking powder
1 tablespoon vanilla extract

Preheat oven to 350º. Butter and spray a 9" pie pan and then set aside. In a small saucepan melt chocolate and butter over low heat until smooth, stirring frequently. Pour into a plastic bowl and set aside to cool. In a large mixing bowl whisk eggs and Splenda® until light colored. Whisk in almond flour, baking powder, and vanilla extract until well combined. Stir in cooled chocolate mixture. Pour into prepared pan and bake 20 minutes. While pie is baking prepare topping.

Peanut Butter Topping:

1/4 cup creamy peanut butter (6 grams carbs per 2 tablespoons)
1 large egg white
1/2 teaspoon liquid Sweet'N Low® sweetener
Chocolate Drizzle (page 19)

In a small bowl whisk all topping ingredients except Chocolate Drizzle until smooth. When pie has baked 20 minutes, remove from oven and carefully spread topping evenly over pie. Return to oven and bake another 8-12 minutes or until set. Topping will look bubbly and foamy until cool. When completely cooled, top with Chocolate Drizzle. Cut into 10 equal pieces. Store covered in the refrigerator. Best when served cold.

10 Servings at 5.9 grams carbs each

Peanut Butter Pie

This one is a family favorite! It's terrific with either the chocolate crust or the peanut butter crust. The difference in carbs is negligible. Decisions, decisions

1 - recipe Chocolate Cookie Crust, (page 90) or
    Peanut Butter Crust (page 91)
Baked and cooled

Topping:
2 tablespoons heavy whipping cream
2 tablespoons butter, softened
1/4 cup creamy peanut butter (6 grams carbs per 2 tablespoons)
2 tablespoons Splenda® sweetener

In a small bowl mix above ingredients until well blended and then set aside.

Filling:
2 cups heavy whipping cream
1 tablespoon sugar-free Jell-O® instant vanilla pudding mix
1/4 cup Splenda® sweetener
1 teaspoon vanilla extract
Chocolate Drizzle (page 19)

In a medium mixing bowl whip all filling ingredients except Chocolate Drizzle with an electric mixer until stiff. Pie will not cut nicely if not whipped stiff. Scrape into cooled crust and spread evenly. Drop peanut butter mixture by small spoonfuls randomly over filling. Swirl into filling with a knife in an attractive fashion as evenly as possible. Top with Chocolate Drizzle. Refrigerate at least 2 hours. Cut into 8 equal pieces. Store covered in the refrigerator.

**8 Servings at 6.3 grams carbs each
with Chocolate Cookie Crust**

**8 Servings at 6.6 grams carbs each
with Peanut Butter Crust**

Pumpkin Spice Cream Pie

Wow – so delicious with the Spice Cookie Crust that you
won't be able to resist this one if you like pumpkin pie.
Even better topped with sweetened whipped cream!

1 - recipe Spice Cookie Crust, (page 91) baked and cooled

Filling:
2 cups heavy whipping cream
2 tablespoons sugar-free Jell-O® instant butterscotch pudding mix
1 1/2 teaspoons ground cinnamon
1/2 teaspoon ground ginger
1/8 teaspoon ground cloves
1/2 cup Splenda® sweetener
1 teaspoon liquid Sweet'N Low® sweetener
1/2 cup solid pack canned pumpkin

In a medium mixing bowl combine all filling ingredients except pumpkin. Whip
with an electric mixer until stiff. Gently fold pumpkin into whipped mixture.
Scrape into cooled crust and spread evenly. Refrigerate at least 2 hours. Cut into
8 equal pieces. Store covered in the refrigerator.

Note: Make sure to count the extra carbs if topping with Sweetened Whipped
Cream (page 78).

8 Servings at 6.7 grams carbs each

Raspberry Cream Cheese Pie

This is so yummy and so few carbs. What a terrific combination adding a dollop of sweetened whipped cream for not only a nice appearance but it also tastes great!

1 - recipe Vanilla Cookie Crust, (page 92) baked and cooled

Filling:
1 - 8 oz. package cream cheese, softened
1/4 cup sugar-free raspberry syrup (0 carbs)
1/4 cup Splenda® sweetener
1 tablespoon low carb raspberry fruit spread (2 grams carbs per
    1 tablespoon)
1 cup heavy whipping cream

In a medium mixing bowl whip cream cheese with an electric mixer until smooth and fluffy. Beat in syrup and Splenda® until well blended. Add fruit spread and cream and whip until stiff. Scrape into cooled crust and spread evenly. Refrigerate at least 4 hours. Cut into 8 equal pieces. Store covered in the refrigerator.

Note: Be sure and count the extra carbs if adding a dollop of Sweetened Whipped Cream (page 78).

8 Servings at 3.5 grams carbs each

Raspberry Mousse Pie

Treat yourself with this light and luscious dessert

1 – recipe Vanilla Cookie Crust, (page 92) or Chocolate Cookie Crust, (page 90) Baked and cooled

Filling:
1 cup boiling water
2 small boxes sugar-free raspberry Jell-O®
1 cup cold water
2 1/2 cups heavy whipping cream
1/3 cup Splenda® sweetener
1 1/2 teaspoons sugar-free Jell-O® instant vanilla pudding mix
Sweetened Whipped Cream (optional)

In a medium plastic bowl dissolve Jell-O® in boiling water, stirring until completely dissolved. Stir in cold water and then refrigerate until syrupy. When Jell-O® is syrupy, whip cream, Splenda®, and pudding mix in a large bowl with an electric mixer until thickened. Add syrupy Jell-O® and continue to whip until very thick. Do not over beat or cream will turn to butter. Spread evenly in cooled crust. Refrigerate at least 2 hours. Cut into 8 equal pieces. Store covered in the refrigerator. Garnish with Sweetened Whipped Cream (page 78) if desired.

Note: Be sure and count the extra carbs if adding the Sweetened Whipped Cream.

8 Servings at 4 grams carbs each with Vanilla Crust

8 Servings at 4.7 grams carbs each with Whipped Cream

8 Servings at 4.6 grams carbs each with Chocolate Crust

8 Servings at 5.3 grams carbs each with Whipped Cream

Rhubarb Cream Pie

Old fashioned goodness in a pie that's actually good for you.
This is a big hit at our house!

Filling:
2 cups fresh rhubarb, diced small
1 cup Splenda® sweetener
1/4 cup Brown Sugar Twin® sweetener
Pinch of salt
1/2 teaspoon xanthan gum
1/2 cup heavy whipping cream
1/4 cup water
3 large egg yolks

Preheat oven to 425°. In a medium bowl whisk dry ingredients together. Whisk in cream, water, and egg yolks until smooth and then set aside. Make Meringue Pie Crust (see below).

1 - recipe Meringue Pie Crust, (page 90) baked 5 minutes at 425° (use egg whites left from filling above). Reduce oven temperature to 325°.

Quickly spread rhubarb evenly over crust because crust will shrink fast. Pour filling mixture over rhubarb and bake 45-55 minutes or until set and lightly browned. Cool in pan on a rack until completely cool.

Topping:
1 cup heavy whipping cream
1/2 teaspoon vanilla extract
3 tablespoons Splenda® sweetener
1/4 teaspoon liquid Sweet'N Low® sweetener

In a small mixing bowl whip all topping ingredients together until thick. Do not over beat or it will turn to butter. Spread on completely cooled pie. Cut into 8 equal pieces. Store covered in the refrigerator. Best when served cold.

8 Servings at 6.5 grams carbs each

Strawberry Chiffon Pie

Light, luscious and summery. This pretty pie hits the spot
after a heavy protein-packed meal. Garnish with
sweetened whipped cream if desired

1 - recipe Vanilla Cookie Crust, (page 92) baked and cooled

Filling:
1 1/2 cups fresh strawberries, washed and hulled, 1/2 cup crushed,
     remaining 1 cup sliced
2 cups heavy whipping cream
2 tablespoons sugar-free Jell-O® instant vanilla pudding mix
1/4 cup Splenda® sweetener
1 teaspoon strawberry extract
Few drops red food color (optional)

In a medium mixing bowl whip all filling ingredients except sliced strawberries
until stiff. Pie will not cut nicely if not whipped stiff. Gently fold in sliced
strawberries. Scrape into cooled crust and spread evenly. Refrigerate at least
2 hours. Cut into 8 equal pieces. Store covered in the refrigerator.

Note: Be sure to count the extra carbs if topping with Sweetened Whipped
     Cream (page 78).

8 Servings at 6 grams carbs each

Triple Chocolate Pie

Lookout chocolate lovers - this is "to die for".
You will love this one!

1 - recipe Chocolate Cookie Crust, (page 90) baked and cooled

Filling:

2 cups heavy whipping cream
3 tablespoons sugar-free Jell-O® instant chocolate fudge or chocolate
   pudding mix
1 tablespoon unsweetened baking cocoa mixed with 1 tablespoon
   boiling water and then cooled
3 tablespoons Splenda® sweetener
1 teaspoon chocolate extract
Chocolate Drizzle (page 19)

In a medium mixing bowl whip all filling ingredients except Chocolate Drizzle with an electric mixer until stiff. Pie will not cut nicely if not whipped stiff. Scrape into cooled crust and spread evenly. Top with Chocolate Drizzle. Refrigerate at least 2 hours. Cut into 8 equal pieces. Store covered in the refrigerator.

8 Servings at 5.2 grams each

Chocolate Cookie Crust
This is so yummy you could eat it without filling

1/2 cup butter, softened (1 stick)
1 cup plus 2 tablespoons Carb Solutions® chocolate shake mix

Preheat oven to 350°. Spray a 9" pie pan and then set aside. In a medium bowl cream butter and shake mix thoroughly. Press dough evenly on bottom and up sides of prepared pan. Use thumb side of hand to press, not fingers. Spray hand to prevent dough from sticking. Bake for 12 minutes. Cool in pan on a rack.

Whole chocolate cookie crust is 13.5 grams carbs

Meringue Pie Crust
Ever so light - the perfect compliment to many different dessert fillings

3 large egg whites
1/2 teaspoon cream of tartar
1/4 cup Splenda® sweetener
1 teaspoon vanilla extract

Preheat oven to 425°. Butter and spray a 9" pie pan and then set aside. In a large deep mixing bowl whip egg whites and cream of tartar with an electric mixer until foamy. Continue beating while gradually adding Splenda®, 1 tablespoon at a time. Add vanilla extract and continue to beat until very stiff and slightly shiny. Spread evenly in prepared pan, building up sides. Bake for 5 minutes. Reduce oven temperature to 300° and continue baking for another 30 minutes. Bake as directed in filling recipe or cool to room temperature and then fill if using an unbaked filling.

Whole meringue pie crust is 7.2 grams carbs

Peanut Butter Crust

If you like peanut butter cookies you will love this crust.
It is terrific with a number of different pie fillings.

6 tablespoons butter, softened
3 tablespoons chunky peanut butter (6 grams carbs per 2 tablespoons)
1 cup plus 1 tablespoon Carb Solutions® vanilla shake mix

Preheat oven to 350°. Spray a 9" pie pan and then set aside. In a medium bowl cream butter and peanut butter thoroughly. Stir in shake mix and mix until well blended. Press dough evenly on bottom and up sides of pan. Use thumb side of hand to press, not fingers. Spray hand to prevent dough from sticking. Bake for 12 minutes or until lightly browned. Cool in pan on a rack.

Whole peanut butter crust is 15.7 grams carbs

Spice Cookie Crust

We love this with many different fillings
but it is extra good with pumpkin filling

1/2 cup butter, softened (1 stick)
1 cup plus 2 tablespoons Carb Solutions® vanilla shake mix
1/4 teaspoon ground cloves
1/2 teaspoon ground ginger
1 1/2 teaspoons ground cinnamon

Preheat oven to 350°. Spray a 9" pie pan and then set aside. In a medium bowl whisk together shake mix and spices. Add butter and cream together thoroughly. Press dough evenly on bottom and up sides of prepared pan. Use thumb side of hand to press, not fingers. Spray hand to prevent dough from sticking. Bake for 12 minutes. Cool in pan on a rack.

Whole spice cookie crust is 11 grams carbs

Vanilla Cookie Crust

Fantastic with virtually any filling and tastes like old-fashioned "sugar cookies"

1/2 cup butter, softened (1 stick)
1 cup plus 2 tablespoons Carb Solutions® vanilla shake mix
1/2 teaspoon vanilla extract

Preheat oven to 350°. Spray a 9" pie pan and then set aside. In a medium bowl cream butter and shake mix thoroughly. Stir in vanilla extract until well mixed. Press dough evenly on bottom and up sides of prepared pan. Use thumb side of hand to press, not fingers. Spray hand to prevent dough from sticking. Bake for 12 minutes. Cool in pan on a rack.

Whole vanilla cookie crust is 7.1 grams carbs.

INDEX

INDEX